Faith, Fighting & Forgiving:
Life Lessons from
THE WALKING DEAD

Susan Lehman

Faith, Fighting, and Forgiving:
Life Lessons from The Walking Dead

Copyright © 2016 by Susan Lehman
All rights reserved.

Cover and Interior Design by Robert Lanphear
www.LanphearDesign.com

ISBN: 978-0-9983026-0-7

Printed in the United States of America

Contents

Acknowledgments

Thank you to everyone who helped with this book. In the world of self-publishing, it was a great relief to have quality assistance with the editing, interior design and cover design. Thank you to all those who read sections of the book as it was being written and offered feedback. Thank you to my mom, for just being a great mom and instilling a passion for learning and spirituality. She, my sisters and niece also love *The Walking Dead*. We often have our own *TWD* debriefings on Mondays, and it is great fun to share this with them. Thank you to the incredible team that brings us *The Walking Dead*, both in comic and television form. Those who do the writing clearly have an instinctive knowledge of human behavior, as well as great storytelling chops. And the actors and production crew bring the words to life in a way that does honor to their craft. Finally, thank you to all the *TWD* fans, who are an integral part of the *TWD* phenomenon. I hope this book will be a small addition to your enjoyment of the show.

Introduction

In a world ruled by the dead, we are forced to finally start living.
–Robert Kirkman, *The Walking Dead, Vol. 1: Days Gone Bye*

The Walking Dead has captured the national imagination to an extent that is rare for any television show. It has scaled the mountain and reached a rarified atmosphere of popularity, and the main characters have achieved iconic status. It has spawned its own talk show, *Talking Dead*, which is the first "aftershow" in television history. There are websites, webisodes, blogs, appearances by the cast at ComiCon, Walker Stalker and other conventions, and a universe of merchandise sales. *The Walking Dead (TWD)* has inspired dolls, books, board games, video games, apps, t-shirts, hats, posters, calendars, crossbows (duh), mugs, figurines, key chains, a book of poetry (yes), playing cards, jackets (wings on the back, of course), hoodies, bras, underwear (such as boxers with "This Isn't a Democracy Anymore" or a women's thong with "Dixon Training Camp" on the little triangle), napkins, tablecloths, diapers (yes), bedspreads, sheets, pillowcases, welcome mats, and a "Don't Open, Dead Inside" beach towel. Everything, it seems, except Emmy awards for acting, writing, or directing. The Emmy folks are clearly also operating only on their brain stems.

We are mesmerized. So why? What does *TWD* have that is so appealing? I think there are two major answers. First is that the show is so amazingly, fantastically well done. The second, and the focus of this book, is that it presents life's dilemmas, questions, and ethical issues in a manner that is more stark and laid bare than in our own world.

There are no distractions or modern baggage—no celebrity dramas, no endless political fighting, no reality shows or junk mail, no Black Friday sales, podcasts, tweets, or other poison-tipped darts of meaningless data that are aimed at us every minute of every day. The bottom-line, core human issues are out in the open.

My own journey to living happily in the land of walkers was belated. You might say I didn't get bitten for a while. I confess that before *TWD*, I had zero interest in zombies or movies about them. I watched George Romero's original 1968 *Night of the Living Dead* ("They're coming to get you, Barbara!") years ago, only because I love movies and it is a classic. I never watched any of the Romero sequels, the *Resident Evil* series, or the *28 Days* movies. I didn't know *TWD* even existed for most of the first three seasons, and I had never read any comic books. Ever.

I was finally infected through another fan, my sister Lynn, who is a gentle but persistent person. She called me during Season 3:

LYNN: *You've got to watch this show.*
ME: *But it's zombies.*
LYNN: *You've got to watch this show!*
ME: *But it's zombies!*
LYNN: *(gently exasperated) It's not about the zombies! You've got to watch this show.*

Did I mention persistence?

ME: *Fiiine.*

The first episode I watched was 401 (which means Season 4, Episode 1), "30 Days Without an Accident," in which Daryl, Tyreese, Sasha, Zack and Bob go on a supply run to a big-box store that has numerous unseen zombies on the weak and rotted roof. Inside, Bob causes a free-standing shelf to fall, and the crash wakes the roof zombies from their "there's nothin' going on and no food around" slumber. They start shambling around mindlessly and fall through the roof onto the unsuspecting group below. It is literally raining zombies. Zombies attack humans, humans spear and smash zombie heads, and I all I can think is, "Yeah, right. It's not about the zombies."

To further my initial dismissal, Chris Hardwick comes on during a commercial break to promote *Talking Dead* and says happily and enthusiastically, "After every episode of *The Walking Dead*, there is always so much to talk about!" I literally burst out laughing. Again, yeah, right. I want *so* much to talk about zombies. There is so much to chew on, so to speak.

I turn off the television, call my sister and say thanks-but-no-thanks. She responds with the admonition that I now understand: "You have to watch it from the beginning!" So (fiiine) I got Season 1 from the library and watched 101, "Days Gone By." To the creators of *TWD*, you had me at Rick's scene in his house.

Rick Grimes, channeled via an incredibly talented Andrew Lincoln, wakes from a coma to find himself in a hospital that looks like a war zone. He goes outside and finds hundreds of bodies in the parking lot, a woman (Bicycle Girl) in a park who is pulling herself along the grass by her arms since her lower half went missing, and no living people.

Still in his hospital gown, Rick walks to his house to find his family, but his wife and son are gone. He looks for them, calls out for them in increasing desperation, and falls into a fetal position on his living room floor, crying. He hits his hand against his forehead, trying to wake himself up, and finally looks at his hand, asking "Is this real?" My walls were coming down. Fast.

The deal was sealed later in the episode by Lennie James, the actor who plays Morgan Jones. Morgan and his son Duane save Rick from a walker and explain to him "what happened and what's going on." After Rick leaves to search for his family, Morgan tries to shoot his walker wife, who is wandering around outside of the house, to put her out of her mindless, carnal misery. He aims his rifle out of a second-floor bedroom window, has her in his sights, and just can't do it. Lennie James did a masterful job of being achingly and tragically torn—knowing it was the right thing to do, wanting to, yelling at his son to stay downstairs, but simply not able to pull the trigger. I watched the rest of Season 1, and I understood my sister's words. It's not about the zombies.

Andrew Lincoln and Lennie James are a small part of the vast sea of talent associated with this show, both in front of and behind the camera. There are absolutely no weak links in the production chain. The people behind the writing, directing, acting, costumes, set design, make-up and every other aspect of work that brings this show together are all solid, creative and capable. Every actor on the show has been excellent (which means congratulations also need to go to the casting staff), from those portraying the main characters down to supporting roles like Noah Emmerich as CDC scientist Edwin Jenner in 106, "TS-19", Michael Raymond James and Aaron Muñoz as Dave and Tony in 208, "Nebraska," Robin Lord Taylor and Brina Palencia as the hippie couple in 404, "Indifference," Christopher Berry as the Savior biker group leader in 609, "No Way Out," John Carroll Lynch as Eastman in 604, "Here's Not Here," and Alicia Witt as Paula in 613, "The Same Boat," among many others. The music is also fabulous. Bear McCrary writes a wonderful score, and the songs chosen have beautifully amplified and defined many scenes. An exceptional team brings *TWD* into our world, and the gratitude of the fans is clear and abundant.

I believe that stories have a spiritual purpose—to share experiences, to bond us together, and to help us understand ourselves, each other, and our world. *TWD* has fulfilled this purpose in spades.

The other reason *TWD* is so popular is within us. It is a yearning we feel for opportunities that modern society doesn't often offer: challenges we can rise to on our own, true connection, and learning what really matters. Watching is a way to vicariously reassess our values after all the window dressing and conveniences are gone.

The first night that Rick finds his family and joins the camp outside Atlanta, they all sit and listen to him tell the story of how he woke up in the hospital and found his way to them. This ritual goes back thousands of years—sitting together around the fire, listening to tales of the hunt or the journey. We hear Dale tell the lesson, offered from father to son, not to become enslaved to time, and we get the wisdom from ages past. During the day, the group gathers in a circle around a fire or the hood of a car to debate future action. Just people, face-to-face. Not at a distance, not via pixels, but real.

We experience this with them, and it appeals to us so much that we replicate it while watching *TWD*. Friends and families gather weekly in front of the glow of the television to experience together, face-to-face, the adventures of this group. Yes, we blog about it, yes, there are memes, and yes, we share our thoughts electronically. But if that was enough, there wouldn't be *TWD* viewing parties—enough of them that *Talking Dead* has held contests for the best ones. We talk about it on Monday mornings at work (during breaks, really, honest), and when we meet someone who is also a devotee, we feel an immediate connection. This is itself a lesson: when we have something we want to share, we can do it electronically for speed, but the thing that truly lights us up is to share it in person. Pixels have their place, but as a tool, not a raison d'être. "I tweet, therefore I am" is no way to live.

There are other lessons for us in the trials of our *TWD* heroes, who I will call the Rickites, and this book presents my thoughts on those lessons. These thoughts reflect my opinions and outlook, and I don't expect everyone to agree with all of them. Or even any of them. Agreement is nice, but disagreement can be healthy and constructive when it spurs conversation and helps us move forward to solve a problem.

There is a great deal of psychology, philosophy and religious commentary in these pages, and *TWD* brings a refreshing perspective to these topics: ordinary people can handle life's issues without "professionals" and "experts." Basic human wisdom and common sense should be celebrated, cherished and nurtured.

Modern culture gives too much authority to "professionals" for handling psychological problems or offering spiritual comfort. Most of us are wiser than we realize, but we don't practice developing and honoring that wisdom. We don't listen to our guts. And the more we disown the validity of our own experiences and what our gut is telling us, the more we will forget how to access our wisdom—or even that we have it within us. There is a place for professionals, but it isn't on a pedestal.

For example, Carol gives Daryl the best advice on how to deal with the death of Beth not because she has a Master of Arts in Social Work with a Special Certification in Grief Counseling, but because she cares about him, she knows him well, and he trusts her. The farmer Hershel runs spiritual rings around the professional pastor, Father Gabriel. And no certificate on the wall for a PhD in Strategic Management would have given Glenn the leadership he developed if it wasn't already there, waiting to come out. No need for letters and titles bestowed by previous "experts." Just a strong spirit, common sense and a good heart. In most cases, a good friend who is person of goodwill can provide answers that are just as valid as those coming from a professional. And the person receiving the advice is free to take it or leave it. They will anyway.

Two final notes. First, this book (which covers the show to the end of Season 6) is one big spoiler. If you haven't watched the show and would like to, I recommend doing that first, unless knowing major plot points ahead of time doesn't bother you. (Although I will add that nothing in this book could possibly do justice to what you will see on the screen.) Second, this commentary is based solely on the television show, with all respect for Robert Kirkman, Tony Moore, Charlie Adlard and the original source. I have now read a couple of the early issues of the comics, but no more than that. My personal preference is to be surprised as the show goes along, rather than read the comics and analyze where the show aligns with or strays from the comic path.

So here is a presentation of lessons we can learn from ordinary, good people in a survival situation. Consume it in good spirits, and bon appétit.

1

We Need the Bearers of Light

It's difficult in times like these: ideals, dreams and cherished hopes rise within us, only to be crushed by grim reality. It's a wonder I haven't abandoned all my ideals, they seem so absurd and impractical. Yet I cling to them because I still believe, in spite of everything, that people are truly good at heart. It's utterly impossible for me to build my life on a foundation of chaos, suffering and death. I see the world being slowly transformed into a wilderness, I hear the approaching thunder that, one day, will destroy us too, I feel the suffering of millions. And yet, when I look up at the sky, I somehow feel that everything will change for the better, that this cruelty too shall end, that peace and tranquility will return once more.

–Anne Frank, *Diary of a Young Girl*,
  Entry dated July 15, 1944

There are still good people, Daryl.
–Beth, 413, "Alone"

I believe we all have Light inside. Like the Quakers and Hindus, I believe that we all carry within us the spark of the Divine. But for most of us there is so much anger, ego, fear, jealousy, ambition, resentment, or other forms of emotional gunk piled on top that it is hard for the light (in lower case from here on) to shine through. I believe in reincarnation, and that the purpose of our soul's journey through lives is to understand and work through these layers of emotions, empathize with others who have faced similar challenges, and ultimately loosen the grip that emotions so often have on us. Emotions are part of our soul's anatomy. Having them available is a gift; clinging to them is not.

It is understandable that we have these built up negative emotions, and that we hold dear to them. We use them as suits of armor to keep our inner vulnerabilities safe. We live in a very difficult world, and a certain amount of armor is necessary. Also, in our world as in *TWD*, everyone has different missions, and some of those missions require good, solid protection.

However, several characters in *TWD* have armor that is thin, or has pockets or openings so their light can get out. They don't excel in physical strength or fighting skills, and they do not offer lessons on how to survive in this world of carnage. Instead, they plant seeds in the hearts of the stronger characters that better times are possible, that better ways of being are possible. In the midst of death, violence, and despair, they testify that there are still things to live for, to hope for, both within ourselves and out in the world. Their stronger friends will remember, and those memories will help them to keep going, and to fight for the right reasons.

In *TWD*, as in our world, it is easy to see the accomplishments of the warriors like Michonne, who keep everyone alive; the hunters like Daryl, who keep people fed; or intellects like Eugene and Reggie, who know how to design and build walls, filter creek water, keep solar panels running and develop recipes for making bullets. On the other hand, it is easy to overlook the gifts of the bearers of light. We like the light bearers—they are often sweet and fuzzy and kind. But we generally don't think of their contributions as tangible and valuable. It's good to remember, especially in hard times, that giving someone a reason to keep going, or helping a person believe in themselves, are very, very valuable gifts.

In *The Walking Dead*, there are five major bearers of light. Four are human: Beth, Bob, Hershel and Tyreese. The fifth is the deer. (I'm guessing *TWD* fans know which deer I mean.)

These four are not saintly. Bob and Hershel battled issues with alcohol, Beth attempted suicide, and Tyreese raged violently against himself and others after Karen was killed. Being a bearer of light doesn't mean you avoid fear, doubt or pain. But even though they suffered and struggled, these four kept their point of view. Wounded, yet still whole. That is one of the mysteries of light. Its promise is not freedom from suffering, but that even if you suffer, you will find yourself again. Your spark will not dim. These four don't need to worry about "coming back," because they never went anywhere. Here is here.

It's not that the stronger characters have not brought light. Certainly Maggie and Glenn have brought light to each other, as have Carol and Daryl. Carl is an irreplaceable light for Rick, and Michonne, Rick, and Carl are all lights for each other. But these characters each have a primary purpose as leaders and warriors (though Carl is still developing; we don't know yet if he will end up a positive force like Glenn, or if he will darken with Negan on the scene), and the Rickites very much need their strength and determination.

One common quality that Beth, Hershel, Bob and Tyreese share is comfort with emotion; they speak freely of their inner experience and outlook. Another commonality is that all four (and the deer) are dead by the end of Season 5. It is not an easy world for the bearers of light. Their purpose is not to survive, but to share the good news and encourage others, while they can, along the way.

Beth

I know you look at me and you just see another dead girl. I'm not Michonne, I'm not Carol, I'm not Maggie. I survived and you don't get it, because I'm not like you or them. But I made it, and you don't get to treat me like crap because you're afraid.
—Beth, 412, "Still"

Beth does die. But after this episode, Daryl will never again think of her as less than fully alive. She helps him change his outlook about himself and others, and they both show us that anger is not a four-letter word;

that there are constructive and healing ways of handling deep anger and grief. This is one of my favorite episodes, despite the lack of flying heads or yards of intestines. It is full of bonding and emotion, as are many of the episodes in the excellent back half of Season 4.

Beth and Daryl end up on the road together after the mid-season finale culminates with the fall of the prison after the Governor's third attack. The Governor is the charming, sociopathic tyrant in a town called Woodbury who will brook no competition from another nearby leader such as Rick. He has already attacked the prison twice. In 408, "Too Far Gone," he makes his final surprise attack, and this time his group includes a former soldier with a tank. As the battle begins, the Rickites pass weapons along to each other and devise a plan to meet and escape together if things "go south." But in the chaos of battle the plan doesn't work, and the Rickites are scattered. They flee the prison in small groups of two or three as numerous walkers amble through the fences and walls that have been demolished by the tank.

Beth and Daryl could not be more opposite. Daryl is the hunter, the warrior, the motorcycle-riding, leather-jacket wearing, crossbow-toting hardass. Beth is the petite blonde teenager who takes care of the infant Judith, writes in her diary (at least during the time of relative calm at the prison), and sings sweet songs in the middle of hell.

Their backgrounds are also worlds apart. Beth grew up on a comfortable, successful farm with a loving family—going on vacations, singing and learning to play piano. Daryl is the child of an abusive father and an alcoholic mother. When his mother died, he was sometimes left alone while his father was off on an alcohol bender for days at a time, and his bigoted, meth-addicted, angry older brother was away in juvenile detention. Daryl adores his brother, Merle, but he doesn't harbor the same rage.

During Beth and Daryl's time together, these worlds collide. They have been through tremendous trauma and loss, and both have anger as a natural result of that. Yes, anger is natural. We've all had things happen to us that made us angry. Emotions are a part of us, and to ignore any of them would be to deny the fullness of who we are. Anger is not inherently bad; it is an internal barometer that something is not right in our lives. Once we acknowledge that we are angry, the key is to express our anger constructively. Here is a list of guidelines that will help do that. Beth and Daryl use these, and we will see their example.

1. Tell yourself that it is okay to express your anger, and do so. Remind yourself that anger is part of our emotional anatomy—it is only suppressing it or expressing it in a hurtful way that makes it destructive. Also, ignoring it at a low level will not make it go away, and it will only grow. You will never find a solution or a relief to your frustration if you can't even express that frustration.

2. If possible, do so directly with the person involved. Sometimes you can't and shouldn't, such as with a boss or teacher or someone who has a position of power over you. And certainly not if the person is abusive or you would risk your emotional or physical safety by confronting them. (And if you are with someone who would be a threat to your physical or emotional safety just for speaking your mind, then you need to get out of that relationship. You deserve better. Truly, you do.) But in many cases—with friends, family, romantic partners, and spouses—it is possible to talk with the person directly. It's just scary because we aren't taught how to do so.

3. Be honest. Own your feelings of anger. So often our instinct is to respond to our hurt and anger by attacking the other person's faults: "You don't know anything," "There you go, eating too much again," or "You can't even hammer a nail without making a mess of it." We unsheathe our claws in defense (social media is now a common outlet for this). Or, we aim our anger sideways at someone who has nothing to do with the source of our anger (social media is a prime pathway for this as well), insulting or attacking the innocent bystander. Such is the human need to retain our emotional balance and regain our lost feelings of power that we let anger come out negatively. But this doesn't solve the

problem, because we aren't really owning our feelings of anger. Then the person we clawed will feel a loss of power, criticize back, and on it goes. The way to break the cycle is to stand your ground, and with strength and openness, express your anger from your heart, and say how the situation or behavior is affecting you. You can be strong without attacking, blaming, or shaming.

4. Allow yourself to be vulnerable if you feel safe enough with the person. Underneath our anger is fear or pain. If you do feel safe (and only then), you can be honest about your fear or how your feelings are being hurt.

5. Express anger at a specific behavior, not at the person as a whole. Saying "You are lazy," or "You're mean," or "You are so selfish" attacks the whole person. It will make them put up defensive walls, it doesn't communicate the actual behavior that bothers you, and it won't solve the problem. It's better to describe the specific behavior, which could be anything from a person not cleaning up their own messes, flirting with others at parties, not appreciating work that you have done, or forgetting something important to you.

6. Offer a solution that you would prefer (which may just be "Stop it."). Communicating constructively about the issue may also open up a dialogue that allows solutions to be found jointly. The married person who flirts could tell people at parties, "Hey, I'm a natural flirt, but I'm married now, and my other half is right over there, and I'll hear about it for days if I don't honor that." That is just one example. Solutions are as diverse as the people who create them.

If your anger is the result of truly horrid acts such as abuse, rape, violence committed against someone you love, or lesser offenses that lasted over a long period of time, it will take more than one conversation to unlock the buckets of pain and anger that weigh down your soul. It can take years of working through it and letting go. There are lots of books on dealing with deep anger (I liked *The Dance of Anger* by Harriet Lerner, PhD), and addressing this topic does merit an entire book. Different methods work for different people, and you can find something that works for you. Again, don't confront anyone if it would risk your physical or emotional safety. But do try to find ways to release your anger, to get it out of you. You deserve a lighter load, and no matter how many years have gone by, no matter how much you try to just get on with your life and lose yourself in the daily needs of work, friends, and family, the pain and anger will still be there if you have avoided them. Time by itself may dull the pain, but it doesn't necessarily heal all wounds.

Here's a test. If you think about the person or event, how does it make you feel? Does it make you anxious? Angry? Does your stomach start hurting? Do you talk about it intellectually, keeping your emotions at a safe distance? Even if you talk about it intellectually, does it bring up a low burn of resentment? All of these are indications that the anger and pain are still in you. Please read, talk to people, and find a constructive way to work it out of you. You deserve better. You deserve healing.

Both Daryl and Beth handle their anger in constructive ways. Beth in particular shows us that it is possible to care about someone, be strong, and express anger in a way that doesn't accuse or blame.

In 410, "Inmates," Beth and Daryl are living in the woods, running from walkers and eating snakes and squirrels. Beth's father Hershel was beheaded by the Governor in front of her, and they have no idea if anyone else they love and care about has survived. Daryl is not speaking; he has completely shut down. Beth has inherited her father's determination and positive outlook, and she wants to find their friends and her sister, Maggie. Daryl reluctantly helps her and they find some tracks in the woods, both human and walker. When they follow the tracks to a clearing, there are walkers dining on dead bodies. It is nobody they know, but it brings Beth to tears.

Back at their camp, in 412, Beth states that she wants a drink, which she has never had because her father was a recovering alcoholic. She leaves and Daryl follows her, but he then takes them in a circle and right back to camp. This brings out her first burst of frustration.

Do you feel anything? Yeah, you think everything's screwed. I guess that's a feeling. So you want to spend the rest of our lives staring into a fire and eating mud snakes? Screw that! We might as well do something! I can take care of myself, and I'm gonna get a damn drink.

This is not some female accusation that he doesn't talk about his feelings enough—it is a true statement that he is letting his negativity stop him from moving forward. Also, in criticizing staying at the camp, she says, "Screw that," not "Screw you." She is addressing the action, not the man as a whole. We can hear anger aimed at us much more readily if we are not being attacked as a person. Daryl has his reasons for shutting down, but she doesn't know them. Yet.

She stomps off, and because he is a decent man who won't leave her out in the forest vulnerable and alone, he follows her again. This time he does help; he takes her to a worn-down house he discovered on a supply run with Michonne, and where he knows exactly what he will find: moonshine.

The house is in disrepair in structure and soul, and mirrors Daryl's childhood surroundings. He knew there would be jars of moonshine in the shed because his father had one just like it.

They play a drinking game of "I Never." She's never shot a crossbow. He's never been out of Georgia. She's never gotten drunk and done something she regretted. He's never been on vacation. But when Beth insinuates that Daryl has spent time in jail, he asks her flatly, "That's what you think of me?" His mood turns sour, fueled by the moonshine, and these two worlds collide. While it appears that this conflict could be a formula for disaster, what we actually witness is a beautiful sequence with lessons on healing pain and anger.

Daryl's anger at his traumatic upbringing has been suppressed. His back still bears the scars of whatever implement his father used on him, but he was powerless to express any anger at the time. Daryl's pain is still there, being in that house stirs it up, and after Beth intimates that he is a criminal, it spills over. He yells at Beth, challenging her privilege and naiveté.

Oh, wait. It's my turn, right? I never, ah, never eaten frozen yogurt. Never had a pet pony! Never got nothin' from Santa Claus! Never relied on anyone for protection before! Hell, I don't think I ever relied on anyone for anything! Never sung out in front of a big group out in public like everything was fun, like everything was a big game! I sure as hell never cut my wrists lookin' for attention!

Just as Beth never said, "Screw you," Daryl never blames her for anything they are experiencing, nor does he talk about who she *is*. Even in mentioning her suicide attempt, he doesn't label her as a person. He simply describes a behavior he doesn't like. Also, underneath the anger is vulnerability. The whole speech is about his own pain and anger from his childhood, and it is the most intimate confession that he has shared with anyone. He is letting Beth into his heart with the truth of what he went through and what he missed.

In 306, "Hounded," Daryl told Carl about how his mother died drinking and smoking in bed, but that was a controlled sharing of facts. It was good and it was mostly for Carl's benefit since Carl had just lost his own mother, but it was not cathartic. Processing pain through brain cells intellectually is nice and it helps, but it is not enough. To be truly healed from such traumatic incidents, pain has to come out of our gut. Tears have to be spilled. So Daryl isn't finished.

A walker approaches the cabin, and Daryl taunts Beth on her inability to defend herself.

Hey, you never shot a crossbow before? I'm gonna teach you right now. Come on!

He goes outside, pulls Beth close to him, shoots around her, and quickly pins the walker to a tree. Beth objects, but he continues using the walker as target practice, shouting predictions of where his arrows will land. But the bearer of light can't stand to torture even a walker. She breaks away, goes to the walker and stabs it in the head.

DARYL: *What the hell did you do that for? We was havin' fun!*
BETH: *No, you were being a jackass! If anyone found my dad...*
DARYL: *Don't! That ain't remotely the same!*

Beth expresses her own honest anger, and she, too, uses specific behavior. There is a big difference between "You *are* a jackass" and "You are *being* a jackass." The first is a statement about the whole person; the second describes a temporary behavior—right now, you are being a jackass.

And Beth is not hostile. She knows Daryl well enough to trust him with her vulnerability, and she is almost in tears. Her father might be a walker, and it hurts her to think of someone taunting him for fun. Their exchange goes on:

DARYL: *What do you want from me, girl?!*

BETH: *I want you to stop acting like you don't give a crap about anything! Like nothing we went through matters! Like none of the people we lost meant anything to you. It's bullshit!*

DARYL: *Is that what you think?*

BETH: *That's what I know.*

DARYL: *You don't know nothin'.*

Here, Daryl asks for a specific solution, and Beth offers one. And she does not say Daryl *is* uncaring. She wants him to stop *acting* like it. She describes a specific behavior she doesn't like.

When we express anger at a behavior, it means that we want the behavior to change. If we want a behavior to change, it means that we still care; that we want the relationship to continue. If we stop expressing anger at a behavior and don't care whether it changes or not, it means that we either no longer care about the relationship, or we feel powerless to have any influence in it.

Beth's outburst also holds a compliment: she knows that Daryl does care about their friends. She knows the shut-down toughness is "bullshit," and she sees beyond it into the warm soul that hurts. Daryl has his own feelings to process about their recent loss, though he isn't quite as instinctively skilled as she is:

DARYL: *No, you don't get it! Everyone we know is dead!*

BETH: *You don't know that!*

DARYL: *Might as well, 'cause you ain't never gonna see them again! Rick…you ain't never gonna see Maggie again!*

While it seems that he is talking about Beth, he is again really working out his own feelings of loss. And once he does, his grief starts to come through. He finally breaks down and pours out his feelings of guilt for not continuing his search for the Governor after the second attack on the prison.

The Governor rolled right up to our gates. Maybe if I wouldn't have stopped lookin'. Maybe 'cause I gave up. That's on me. And your dad…maybe, maybe I coulda done something.

And here is the crux of why Daryl shut down; he feels responsibility for the attack and all the tragedy that it brought, including Hershel's death. And now he is on the road with Hershel's daughter. No wonder he couldn't talk to her.

But because Beth worked through her own anger honestly, she can let it go and allow her compassion to rush in. She runs over and hugs him, and they both stand there, next to the walker pinned to the tree, grieving.

In the calm after the storm, they sit on the porch of the moonlit cabin, and Daryl reveals to Beth what he has hidden from everyone else—that before the world fell apart, his place in it was pointless. His days were aimless, spent getting drunk or high and playing second fiddle to his older brother. Here, Beth offers him another gift. She sees the Daryl who has blossomed with his new friends, and she affirms him and the positive qualities he has found within himself.

BETH: *You gotta stay who you are, not who you were. Places like this, you have to put it away.*

DARYL: *What if you can't?*

BETH: *You have to. Or it kills you.*

She puts her hand over her heart.

BETH: *Here.*

In turn, Beth admits to Daryl her own naiveté. She thought they would live normal lives at the prison, with picnics and birthdays, and that her dad would live a long life and die peacefully. She tells Daryl, "That's how unbelievably stupid I am."

And now that Daryl has released his own pain, he can forgive what he recently mocked, and he affirms her hopes, letting her know, "That's how it's supposed to be."

Beth's final gift to Daryl in this episode is to help him find a way to put his beginnings behind him. It is late, and Daryl says they should go inside the house. With a mischievous smile and a gentle chuckle, Beth counters that they should burn it down. She knows, with no degree or certificate, and relying on nothing more than her own silver-winged light intuition, that burning down the house that embodies Daryl's past would be radically healthy. Daryl's response is simple. "We're gonna need more booze."

They splash the remaining jars of moonshine all over the walls and ceiling of the house, go outside, light a rolled-up newspaper and throw it. Bathed in the light of the conflagration, Beth raises a triumphant middle finger to the burning house. She taps Daryl playfully on the arm, and he joins her in the third-digit salute, giving his former life the good riddance it deserves. All this is done in a beautiful sequence to The Mountain Goats' song, *Up the Wolves*. It's a wonderful catharsis for Daryl. As they walk away from the house, with the camera close on Daryl, he has the smallest of smiles.

Yes, some emotional problems are difficult enough to require a professional. (The character of Lizzie is testament to that.) And certainly I am not advocating returning to childhood homes and putting them to flames. But we can reclaim our ability to heal ourselves and others. We can stop our pain from dominating our lives, or at least diminish it to the point that it is relegated to the woven fabric of our past, but isn't debilitating. It takes identifying and owning our anger and pain, and expressing honest feelings about incidents in a constructive, specific, and non-judgmental way. Really, it's not rocket science. Scary, yes. But not rocket science.

Beth isn't finished. Once Daryl has worked through his anger and pain, he is ready to receive a more positive view of people. In 413, they see a house at the far end of a cemetery, fair game for food and supplies. Beth suggests that maybe someone still lives there, and Daryl assures her that if so, he will take care of them; meaning he will contain, hurt, or kill them. It is an assumption of danger, and Beth responds with her message of light, "There are still good people, Daryl."

The house was a funeral home before the apocalypse, with caskets in a front room and a guest sign-in book by the entry. In the basement, they find a walker laid out on a table with makeup applied to half of its (his) face, as if in preparation for a funeral in the "before" time. Daryl berates the effort, but Beth immediately sees the humanity in it.

> *It's beautiful. Whoever did this cared. They wanted these people to get a funeral. They remembered these things were people, before all this. They didn't let it change them in the end. Don't you think that's beautiful?*

Back upstairs, the kitchen cupboards contain jars of peanut butter, jelly, diet soda and pickled pigs' feet, all in neat rows and free of dust, confirming that someone does live there. They take down jars for a meal, and as they dine on the "white trash brunch," Daryl suggests that they can stay there a while and wait for the person to come back, saying, "Maybe…they may be nuts, but maybe it'll be alright."

Daryl has been affected by this lovely and persistent bearer of light— as it turns out, a little too much. He forgets his basic nature as a warrior, which brings out another important lesson: be yourself.

As Beth and Daryl eat, they hear a dog bark. This same dog came to the front door earlier, and at that time Daryl left the kitchen tense, anticipating battle with his crossbow at the ready. He peeked between the strips of wood nailed over the door windows and opened it cautiously. Only when he saw there were no walkers did he open the door fully, and the scared, hungry mutt ran away.

This time, assuming it is only the dog, Daryl saunters to the front door, casually opens it without looking and a crowd of walkers pushes past him and invades the house. Daryl yells to Beth to run out the back door, but by the time he defeats the walkers and comes out of the house, she is gone. Only her purse is left lying on the ground.

Daryl got "infected" by Beth's optimism, forgot his role and let his guard down. If in your core you are a warrior or a leader or a strategist or an intellect, it is good to hear and remember the lessons from the bearers of light, but don't try to become one. It won't work, and you will compromise your primary abilities and purpose.

Similarly, bearers of light shouldn't try to be warriors. Beth tried to be a warrior in 508, "Coda," ineffectively stabbing the Grady Memorial Hospital leader, Dawn, in the shoulder with very small scissors. Her reasons were noble, but it resulted in her death.

There is a difference between trying to be the best *you* possible, and trying to be someone else. We can be content with who we are and the gifts we have to offer. Society needs people in all different roles.

Daryl will never see Beth again until the day she dies. Does he remember everything she taught him? Does he remember her faith in people in 511, "The Distance," when the Rickites are in the barn debating whether or not to trust Aaron, the Alexandria recruiter? Possibly. (Only Norman Reedus knows for sure.)

When Beth does die, Daryl and the rest of the group grieve deeply; they understand that they have lost one who was pure of heart. But her gifts of song, light and hope can't be taken away. In remembering her, they remember that there are still good people in the world, and that we can become better people, ourselves. She left a wonderful legacy.

Bob

Nightmares end. They shouldn't end who you are.
—Bob, 503, "Four Walls and A Roof"

Bob's light message is that we need each other. When fed with the nourishment of human connection, Bob can look out at the apocalypse and see not unending horror, but only a long, dark tunnel that he knows has a light at the end, even if it isn't visible now. He is the member of the Rickites closest to being an outright philosopher, and he teaches that staying together is the best option. Not just for survival, but because together is the best way to reach for a higher purpose. And because without other people, life becomes one lonely, despairing, barely draggable step after another. He knows. He endured it.

Bob survived the fall of two other groups. His survival during his time alone on the road speaks highly of his skills—but not as a warrior. When we see Michonne alone (without her walker camouflage), she easily cuts down walkers with her *katana*. Heads split and fly when she is around. When Bob is alone, his strategy is avoidance: hiding behind a tree with barely any life in his eyes; lodging thick sticks into the opening of an old root cellar in the side of a hill to act as bars while he sleeps inside; or lying on the top of a deserted eighteen-wheeler truck with undead cannibals flowing past him on the road below.

When Glenn and Daryl meet Bob walking alone on the road, they ask him the three questions the Rickites have developed for all strangers: How many walkers have you killed? How many people have you killed? Why? Satisfied with his answers, Glenn invites Bob to join them and asks if he has any questions. He doesn't, telling them, "It doesn't matter who you are." It reveals how much he needs companionship. He is with people again. That is enough.

(Personally, I don't believe Bob's response. I believe he believes it at the time. But he is a good person, and if it had turned out that the Rickites were predators who hurt or took advantage of people, I think he would have left despite the daunting prospect of being alone again. He is not someone who could stay with that kind of group. Just my opinion.)

Bob's light comes out fully after the fall of the prison while he is on the road with Maggie and Sasha. It is mostly aimed at Sasha, both because he is attracted to her romantically, and because she needs his light. The bearers of light and the people who need them tend to find each other.

On the road, Maggie's first priority is to find Glenn, who got separated from her during the prison battle, and she is willing to go alone to find him. Sasha insists that they can't split up, but she wants to focus on their own needs: safe shelter and food. Bob agrees that they must stay together, but he wants to help Maggie; he wants to reach for more than mere survival. And by that, he shows his trust that they will find the means for survival along the way.

Sasha is afraid, Maggie is not. Maggie got separated from the man she loves and is determined to find him. Sasha also got separated from someone she loves—her brother Tyreese—but she never even mentions him. It's not that Sasha and Tyreese aren't close. In 401, Sasha gives everyone, including Tyreese, firm directions and a reminder to stay in formation as they enter the Big Spot. There is a smiling exchange that shows their warm relationship.

> TYREESE: *Was there ever a time when you weren't the boss of me?*
> SASHA: *You had a few years before I was born.*

Yet now, not knowing if he is alive, Sasha retreats emotionally and wants to aim only for personal survival. But she is outnumbered, and in 413, the three of them walk together all day, looking for Glenn. That night, while Bob and Sasha think Maggie is asleep, Sasha tells Bob how she truly feels. "Odds are Glenn is dead. Odds are we will be too. That's the reality."

Maggie overhears this and leaves before they wake up. Bob insists they should catch up to her, and Sasha gives in again. As she and Bob walk together, she can't understand his positive mood.

> SASHA: *You have been grinning since we left the prison in one piece. If you're so happy to be alive, then why are we walking into the heart of darkness?*
> BOB: *It's not about me being alive.*
> SASHA: *Do you even know why you're smiling?*
> BOB: *Oh, yeah. I'm not alone.*

Bob's lesson is clear: being together and taking risks is more life-affirming than being alone and surviving.

They pass a sign with a message written in walker blood: "Glenn, go

> ## Great Moments
>
> In 415, "Us," Abraham, Eugene, Rosita, Tara and Glenn are walking together when Glenn sees another walker-blood message: "Glenn, go to Terminus. Maggie, Sasha, Bob." It is his first proof that Maggie is alive, and he immediately breaks into a run. The close camera shot on his face and the joyous smile that breaks out are fabulous. Great directing, great camera, great acting. Steven Yeun shoulda gotta Emmy long ago.

to Terminus. Maggie." They've seen signs to Terminus before. Bob and Sasha are on the right track (literally) to finding Maggie, and continue toward Terminus.

That night, Bob continues to try to help Sasha. With the clear vision of a light bearer, he sees through her talk about food and shelter into her true fear.

> *Why do you think Tyreese is dead? If Tyreese were alive, he'd go for Terminus. I know you know that. So why do you think he's dead? Or are you just too afraid to find out if he is or not?*

But Sasha isn't ready yet. On their second day without Maggie, they come to a crossroads with a two-story building, and Sasha says they should stop there and live safely on the second floor. Bob refuses. He keeps challenging her, and tells her how he was afraid of losing another group when he first got to the prison.

> **Bob:** *Bad things happened because I was scared. They didn't need to. I didn't need to be afraid. Now, we get to Terminus, and Tyreese isn't there, it doesn't mean he's dead. You don't need to be afraid.*
> **Sasha:** *I am not afraid!*

She is still not convinced. She asks Bob to stay again, but Bob is true to his beliefs and follows Maggie's path—the path of the brave woman, the one reaching for a higher purpose. So he goes, and Sasha gets her wish; she is in a safe place where she can fortify. But instead of being

Great Music

Maggie and Sasha's reunion with Bob is one of the many *TWD* scenes that is wonderfully enhanced by the music. Lee DeWyze's *Blackbird Song* is first played when we saw Bob alone, and it is repeated here. With its bluesy, country violins underneath and long vocal stretch on top, it beautifully accentuates the reunion of these three as they hug and are a team once again.

content, when she gets to the second floor, she has to fight tears. It seems she is learning quickly—preserving your life in solitude is worse than risking it with others.

But before Bob and Sasha got to the crossroads, Maggie had changed her mind about going it alone and stopped there ahead of them. She is sleeping on the ground among several walkers she killed (camouflage, of course), and Sasha looks out the second floor window and sees her. She puts her hand on the window, which immediately falls out and crashes down, waking up Maggie and drawing more walkers. Sasha runs outside, they defeat the walkers, and Maggie confronts Sasha's fear directly, just as Bob did.

I'm not giving up, but I need your help. 'Cause I can't do it by myself. And even if I catch up to Bob, we can't do it alone. And I thought that I couldn't ask you to risk your life, but I can. 'Cause I know what you'd be risking it for. And it isn't just Glenn. I get that you're afraid.

And finally, Sasha speaks her own emotional truth.

I am. I am afraid.

As with other times in *TWD* (and in our lives), once emotional truth is spoken out loud to a person who cares, the person who was stuck can move forward. Sasha has the loving support of two strong friends and she has been honest about her fear, so now she can face it.

MAGGIE: *We can get there.*
SASHA: *I know. So let's go get Bob. And let's get there.*

"There" is Terminus, and all the Rickites do get there. But Terminus is the home of a group of cannibals. Even here, Bob is a bearer of light.

In 501, "No Sanctuary," the Rickites are forced into an empty train car (there are several Nazi references in Terminus), gas is dropped through the ceiling and Bob, Rick, Daryl and Glenn are dragged out and end up bound and gagged, on their knees in front of a stainless-steel trough, watching and waiting as the four men next to them have their throats cut and fall forward bleeding into the trough. Desperate, Bob begs the Terminus leader to remove his gag and let him talk.

> *You don't have to do this! We told you there's a way out of all of this. You just have to take a chance! We have a man who knows how to stop it. He has a cure. We just have to get him to Washington. You don't have to do this, man. We can put the world back to how it was!*

Bob shares messages of hope, even with the grisly leader of Terminus. But his light can't penetrate this level of darkness. Gareth puts the gag back on and answers amiably, "Can't go back, Bob."

Great Moments

At the Terminus trough, Gareth removes Rick's gag and asks him about the contents of a bag the Rickites buried outside the Terminus fence. When Gareth holds a knife to Bob's eye, Rick offers a list of weapons, including a red-handled machete, and promises Gareth, "That's what I'm gonna use to kill you." Even when he is tied up and moments away from death, our warrior-leader is so steady, his gaze so casually certain, that a small moment of doubt flashes in Gareth's eyes before he replaces the gag and smiles. Great stuff.

Thanks to a herd of invading walkers and Carol's fireworks rocket shot into the Terminus oil tank, the Rickites escape and battle out of Terminus. The group, flung apart when the prison fell, is fully reunited. Daryl rushes to Carol and hugs her for dear life, crying and putting his head on her shoulder. Carol leads the group to a Terminus perimeter shack and reunites Rick and Carl with Judith, who they thought was dead. And Sasha is reunited with her brother and finally warms up to Bob—not only because Tyreese is alive after all, but because Bob saw what she was really feeling and didn't let her hide from it.

The Rickites are more bonded and stronger for their experiences, and they know it. In 502, "Strangers," they walk through the forest, staying in close formation with weapons in hand, Rick and former soldier Abraham talking over plans.

Bob and Sasha walk next to each other, relaxed and happy. Now that Sasha has battled through her fear, she is ready to receive more positive messages. It is true for us, too. Fear, anger, jealousy, grief, or other negative emotions don't just block our light from getting out, they also block light from getting in. Positive possibilities can't get through the static. But now they can for Sasha, and Bob shares his lighter side with the verbal game, "The Good Out of the Bad."

SASHA: *Wet socks.*
BOB: *Cool feet.*
SASHA: *Mosquito bites.*
BOB: *Itching reminds you you're alive.*
SASHA: *Danger around every corner.*
BOB: *Never a dull moment.*

It's just a game, and it makes her laugh. Laughter is a valuable commodity in the middle of hell, and as a bearer of light, Bob is just doing his job. His reward? Kisses that are happy and mutual.

But Sasha is not his only target, and now he aims at a tougher subject: Rick. He wants Rick to agree with Abraham's plans to go to Washington, DC, where the scientist (they think) Eugene can cure the virus (they think). For Bob, choosing DC is choosing hope and working together for the highest possibility, rather than staying safe and isolated. Affirming hope is part of "coming back," and Bob is going to promote that idea with Rick as much as he did with Sasha. He talks to Rick in 502 as they are walking to a food bank near Father Gabriel's church, but Rick hasn't decided.

> BOB: *I know. That's cool. But you've seen Abraham in action. He's going to get there, and Eugene's going to cure all this, and you're gonna find yourself in a place where it's like it used to be. And if you let too much go along the way, that's not gonna work, 'cause you're gonna be back in the real world.*
> RICK: *This is the real world, Bob.*
> BOB: *Nah. This is a nightmare, and nightmares end. I'm sorry. I'm callin' it. Washington's gonna happen. You're gonna say yes.*

It will be Bob's last supply run. He is bitten by a walker under three feet of slimy water in the food bank basement. Rick does say yes later that night at the church, no doubt influenced both by Bob's words and by Abraham's speech (only Andrew Lincoln knows for sure). Though Bob is not long for this world, he has done his job. He has convinced the leader to reach for the sky.

To the last, Bob's light shines. Even after all his tragedies—losing his first two groups, being alone, losing the prison, being bitten by a walker and the Terminians—he still shares light on his deathbed at the church. As the group gathers to say their goodbyes, he calls Rick over to offer his last messages to the warrior-leader, reminding him of the highest and best in himself.

> *Before the prison, I didn't know if there were any good people left. ... You took me in, 'cause you took people in. It was you, man. What I said yesterday, I ain't revising it. Even in light of current events. Nightmares end. But they shouldn't end who you are.*

The last person to sit with Bob is Sasha. Even while only half-conscious, he is smiling. She again doesn't understand, and asks him why. His response, as he dies, is still about the people he loves.

Random Thought

I think Sasha has the right idea in hunting walkers. In my opinion, in order to reclaim the world after the zombie apocalypse, five things have to happen. (1) You have to defeat the predator humans, (2) You have to get an army of Rickite positive types to systematically search out and kill all the walkers in a given area, (3) You have to expand that area, (4) Since the virus is inside everyone, rituals have to be developed that include stabbing in the head for all deaths, and (5) Every effort has to be made to ensure that nobody dies alone, ever. Which is kind of nice, anyway. Bob would never want anyone to die alone.

I think I was dreaming, and I think you were smiling back at me in the dream. Yeah. That's it.

And they are his last words. Sasha asks him what is the good that comes out of this bad, but he dies before he can answer.

Bob's influence on Sasha will last beyond his death, though it will be a rough road for her, because Tyreese dies soon after this. Overflowing with rage and grief, Sasha becomes reckless and self-destructive. When the group gets to Alexandria, she can't fit in. She yells at the sheltered Alexandrians about their trite concerns over pasta makers and what her favorite food might be. She isolates herself, asking for multiple shifts on the watchtower and shooting any walkers that approach. She finally goes outside the walls alone to hunt them, acting as if she wants to commit suicide-by-walker and take out as many as possible in the process. At her lowest, Sasha trips and falls into a pit that she dug for the walkers she has killed. Rather than climbing out, she lays down on top of them and stares up at the sky. Just one barely living soul among the dead.

In 516, "Conquer," she goes to Father Gabriel and tells him she isn't sure she wants to live. Father Gabriel is fighting his own demons so he cannot help, and instead berates her and tells her she doesn't deserve to be alive. She screams back, knocks him down, and aims her rifle at him. It is only Maggie's entrance that averts a catastrophe.

Sasha could have committed suicide alone. But she didn't—she reached out for help. She just didn't know that Father Gabriel was also despondent. Perhaps her time with Bob and his love and his lessons reminded her to hold on to any sliver of hope. (Only Sonequa Martin-Green knows for sure.)

After this incident, Sasha stops isolating herself. She accepts being part of the group—on her own terms. She still channels her rage by fighting the walkers, but as part of a team. In 601, "First Time Again," she volunteers to be part of the ambitious plan to draw a huge herd of walkers away from Alexandria. She tells Abraham, "Doing something as big as this? That's living." She is a fellow warrior now, fighting with others for a higher cause—the return of a world where the bearers of light can live again.

Bob is still smiling. He always knew that good would come out of the bad.

Hershel

We got this far somehow; you can believe somehow. Now we all have jobs here. That one's yours.
—Hershel to Glenn, 403, "Isolation"

Hershel Greene is not a bearer of emotional light. He is practical. He represents hope in action, the building of community and keeping faith by keeping going. He is stability and wisdom, handing down skills from generation to generation and honoring families. He blesses *TWD*'s first apocalyptic couple, Maggie and Glenn. He provides for friends and family through knowledge of the earth, from gardening and raising chickens to gathering wild elderberries for a natural flu remedy. Finally, as Rick's mentor he offers both support and challenge, and insists that maintaining humanity in an inhumane world is both possible and necessary.

Rick meets his mentor after asking God for help. In 201, "What Lies Ahead," the Rickites find a church while looking for Carol's missing twelve-year-old daughter, Sophia. Sophia is not there, and only walkers sit in the pews. The Rickites easily dispatch the walkers and leave the church. But Rick goes back in, goes to the altar, faces the statue of Christ and submits a request.

> *The thing is we...I could use a little something to help keep us going. Some kind of acknowledgement, some indication I'm doing the right thing. ...Hey, look, I don't need all the answers, just, just a little nudge, a sign! Any sign'll do.*

Rick's prayer is answered, but not with a sign. He gets Hershel, and his son Carl has to be accidentally shot by Hershel's farmhand in order to bring them together. The road to answered prayers is not necessarily clear and comfortable. Sometimes a complicated chain of events is required and the result isn't what we expected. We just can't see the whole picture. But Rick's prayer was answered, because Hershel is the person who shows him how to keep going and keep doing the right thing.

Hershel is invaluable when we first meet him—he saves Carl's life. But he can't take on his new mentor role until two things happen. First, he has to release his misguided thinking that the walkers are just people who are "sick," which happens when he sees Shane shoot a walker three times in the chest and stomach with no effect whatsoever.

Second, he has to give up his position as "lord of the manor" of his farm, which happens when a large herd invades in 213, "Beside the Dying Fire." Hershel futilely uses a shotgun against the undead horde taking over his land, and Rick physically pulls him away to save him from being attacked.

HERSHEL: *It's my farm!*
RICK: *Not anymore! Come on!*

At the end of the episode, Hershel's farm is in flames and overrun with walkers. Everyone has fled in different directions, and Hershel is with Rick and Carl. They drive to the highway where the Rickites were caught in a jam of abandoned cars (and where poignantly, a message for Sophia remains), hoping that others will have the same idea. When no one else is there, Carl wants to go back to the farm to get his mother and challenges Rick:

> *Why are we running? What are you doing? It's Mom! We need to get her, and not be safe a mile away!*

Carl stomps off when Rick kneels down to comfort him, and it is here that Hershel begins his mentoring. He knows that returning to the farm is not an option, and that being out in the open on the highway is also dangerous.

> HERSHEL: *Rick, you've got to get your boy to safety. I'll wait here for my girls and the others. I know a few places. We'll meet up at one of them later.*
> RICK: *Where? Where's safe? We're not splitting up.*
> HERSHEL: *Please. Keep your boy safe.*

Rick objects, wanting to stay together and wait there for the others. As walkers start approaching, Hershel presses again.

> HERSHEL: *I don't know how much longer we can stay here.*
> CARL: *I'm not leaving without Mom.*
> RICK: *So we're just gonna walk away, not knowing if my wife, your girls are still out there? How do we live with that?*
> HERSHEL: *You've only got one concern now. Just one. Keeping him alive. Nature may be throwing us a curve ball, but that law is still true.*

Hershel's lesson: you are a father before you are a leader. And if you are a father whose child is in danger, you are a father above all else.

The difficult decision to leave the highway is averted when Daryl and Carol drive up, then Glenn and Maggie, and finally Lori, Beth and T-Dog (gotta love those heartwarming *TWD* reunions). After hugs and sharing intel on what happened to the missing members of the group (Shane, Patricia, Jimmy and Andrea), they drive in a caravan

Great Writing

With no dialogue in the first five minutes of 301, "Seed," we see a bonded and seasoned group enter an abandoned house in search of food. Rick, Daryl, T-Dog and Carl enter first and clear the house of walkers, followed by Maggie and Glenn as back-up. Rick finally whistles an all-clear out the front door, and those who are most vulnerable—a now very pregnant Lori (our visual indication of how much time has passed), Beth, Carol and Hershel—come in last. The only food they get is an owl that Daryl shoots. When Carl brings out cans of dog food from a kitchen cabinet and starts to open one, they are all dejected. Rick will have none of this; he takes the can and throws it aside. It is an important lesson—they are not animals. When T-Dog spots a group of walkers coming toward the house, they all run out the back door, get in their cars (Maggie quickly grabs an axe leaning against the side of the house), and they drive off. All done in silence. Great writing. Great acting. Shoulda gotta Emmy. Really.

away from the farm. Hershel's admonition isn't put to the test, but he has begun his role as Rick's mentor and will continue to both support and challenge Rick.

When one car runs low on gas, Rick wants to stop and make camp for the night. But some in the group are worried because they don't know where the herd is heading. They want to keep moving, and the group starts arguing. It is now that Hershel officially begins his support of Rick as the group leader, and he states emphatically, "Everyone stop panicking and listen to Rick."

Rick's position as leader is sealed with his "This isn't a democracy anymore" speech, one of the amazing monologues brought to us by Andrew Lincoln (who should have Emmys lining a shelf in his house). Rick may have declared himself sole leader, but he is a capable leader who listens to the advice of his people, and the group survives a winter on the road together.

A good mentor will offer challenge as well as support. A mentor is a truth teller. There are constructive ways to do this, but any mentor worth their salt will let their mentee know when they are wrong as well as when they are right. Hershel does both.

After the Rickites find a prison and move into this protected facility, Lori dies in childbirth and Rick starts "wandering Crazy-town," as Glenn puts it. He hears voices on a dead phone line and sees visions of Lori in the prison. He follows her as she moves out to the prison yard and beyond the prison fences. When he finally reaches her, she puts her hand lovingly on his cheek, soothing him. He stays out there, wanting to be near whenever she appears.

The problem is that there is nobody who can match Rick's leadership, and the group feels the loss as the threat from the Governor looms. In

Hallucinations, Visitations, or Visions?

Rick's visions of Lori and Tyreese's visions at his death have been referred to by some fans as "hallucinations." Even Rick says, "I know it isn't her," but I disagree with Rick. I believe in a soul and an afterlife and that spirits can visit us, which is what happened to Rick and Tyreese. Visions can also be an unexplained mystical experience, as with Daryl's vision of Merle in 205, "Chupacabra." For me, the distinction is that hallucinations are random. Hallucinations are what you experience while on LSD or other drugs—walls melting, bugs crawling on your skin, etc. They do not provide you with support or lessons; they are not images of anyone you knew or loved. The experiences that Rick, Daryl and Tyreese had helped them through difficult situations. Whether visits from spirits or a vision, they are gifts from the Universe.

310, "Home," Hershel goes to the fence, calls Rick over, tells him they need him and asks if there is anything he can do. Rick, tired and pale, confesses to his mentor that he has been seeing Lori and that he wants to stay out there until he understands what the visions mean. Hershel gently urges him to come back in and get some rest.

Rick rejects the request. But he has unburdened the story of his experiences to his mentor, and once this emotional truth is shared, he can begin to move forward. This happens very quickly, and moments later he has to fight again as the Governor attacks the prison by ramming a truck through the prison gate, opening the back door and releasing walkers into the yard. This was the extent of the Governor's plan for now, and once the walkers are out, he and his soldiers leave.

In 311, "I Ain't a Judas," the Governor's former henchman, Merle, assures the group that the Governor will be back.

> *That truck through the fence thing—that's just him ringing the door-bell. You might have some thick walls to hide behind, but he's got the guns and the numbers. And if he takes the high ground around this place, shoot, he could just starve us out if he wanted to.*

The group debates whether to abandon the prison or stand and fight, but Rick still wants to avoid leadership and walks away as arguments start. Hershel is out of patience, and he yells at Rick in front of the group:

> *Get back here! You're slipping, Rick. We've all seen it. We understand why, but now is not the time. You once said this isn't a democracy; now you have to own up to that. I put my family's life in your hands. So get your head clear and do something!*

It is a direct and public challenge that only Hershel (at that point) could make, and it will not be the last one. Hershel confronts Rick again when preteen Carl is dangerously eager to use his gun. Carl is not yet old enough to realize the consequences of firing his weapon, with tragic results.

In preparation for the Governor's second attack, the Rickites plan to lure the Governor's people into the prison basement where walkers still lurk in the dark. Those not directly involved will hide in the woods away from the fray, and Carl resents being assigned to this group.

The plan works. The Governor's inexperienced people encounter the walkers and beat a hasty retreat off the prison grounds. One of them, a teenage boy, runs into Hershel and Carl in the woods. The young man aims a gun at them, but Hershel simply demands that he hand over his weapon, and the scared boy is happy to comply. He is relinquishing his gun when Carl shoots him.

In 316, "Welcome to the Tombs," Hershel tells Rick about the incident. Rick wants to defend Carl, saying he must have thought it was necessary, but Hershel is insistent. "Rick! I'm telling you, he gunned that kid down."

Hershel knows that even (or especially) in the worst of times, there are still rules that must be followed if you hope to maintain any sense of humanity and civilization. He makes Rick remember these rules, even when Rick's own son is the one who broke them.

Carl is defiant when Rick confronts him about shooting the boy. But Rick heeds Hershel's admonitions, takes Carl's gun away and pulls him back from going on supply runs. (It is the *TWD* version of being grounded.)

Even after this, Carl isn't finished with his trigger-happy phase. Hershel deals with him directly during the deadly flu epidemic, when Carl insists on going with Hershel, gun in hand, to gather elderberries as a natural remedy.

While they are in the woods, a lone walker approaches. She stepped into an animal trap somewhere along the way, and drags it mindlessly along clamped to her leg. It makes her slow (even more than the usual walker-slow), so she is no threat. But Carl still raises his gun. If he had fired, it wouldn't have mattered so much this time. Killing a walker is a mercy, and the gun's silencer means no other walkers would be drawn by the shot. But Hershel still objects, telling Carl calmly, "Don't. You don't need to."

Carl clearly wants a piece of the action, but Hershel doesn't let him give in to the tendency to go for his gun as a first response. He knows

Random Thought

I think that Carl's reason for being anxious to use his gun isn't because he is hardened; it is because he wants his father's blessing as part of the team protecting the group. The logic for this comes from 405, "Internment," in which a herd of walkers are pushing down the prison fence. Almost everyone either has the flu or is helping those who do. Maggie and Rick try to fortify the fence, but Maggie leaves when they hear gunshots coming from the cell block. Rick goes to Carl and asks for his help, and it is music to Carl's ears. They start propping up the fence with logs, but the logs don't hold and the walkers pour through. They fall back to an inner courtyard, grab automatic weapons from a laundry tub and Rick teaches Carl on the fly: "Magazine goes in here, release this here. Make sure it latches. Pull back the operating rod, the rounds speed up. Keep squeezing the trigger for rapid fire, okay?…You shoot or you run; don't let them get close."

Carl stands side by side with his father, taking down the walkers. When Rick has to replace a clip and it jams, Carl shoots a walker that gets too close to Rick and tosses his father a new clip. Rick looks at Carl, and we see on his face in that one moment that his entire view of his son has just changed. Carl had his back. And Carl got what he wanted so much—his father asked for his help, and he was able to provide it.

The next morning, Carl jogs to catch up with his father on the way to the prison garden, saying, "Hey! You didn't wake me up." He wants to help with the farming, now. He's been accepted by Rick as part of the team, and he has calmed down.

that if Carl grows up hardened, he could lose himself in these tragedies. He could become "too far gone."

With the elderberries gathered, Hershel is willing to risk his own life by going into the quarantine area to administer the elderberry tea. He shows positive determination that doesn't give in to despair or self-pity.

Sasha and Glenn go with Hershel on his rounds despite being weak with the flu. Hershel insists that they move any bodies and perform the stab in the head away from the other flu victims, so they won't see this potential fate. His concern is for the health of his patients, not just in body but also in spirit.

When they arrive at an isolated room and are ready to prevent the turn for one victim, Lizzie comes to the doorway and asks what they are doing. Hershel doesn't want her to see it, either, and tells her to get his copy of *Tom Sawyer* and read it. He reiterates his refrain, "We've all got jobs to do. That one's yours."

He tries to keep Glenn and Sasha's spirits up with bad jokes, and finally, senior citizen and lame though he is, he fights a walker to reclaim a respirator so he can use it for Glenn. And Hershel doesn't get sick, despite going into the ward. His death doesn't come from a germ.

Hershel is the first person to voice that it is possible to "come back" from the trauma of the apocalypse. In 401, Rick goes into the woods to check the snares they have set for animals. He meets a woman (actress Kerry Condon), who tricks him into coming to her camp, where her husband, Eddie, is a walker. She asks Rick whether he thinks you get to "come back" from these experiences, and she is the first character to pose this question. She tries to kill Rick to feed him to Eddie, but Rick easily throws her off. Having failed to kill Rick, she stabs herself in the stomach and begs him to let her "turn" so she can be like Eddie. As she dies, she answers her own question between shallow gasps: "You don't...you don't get to come back...you don't get to come back... from...things...you don't..."

Rick tells Hershel about this encounter, concerned about his own time lost at sea when Lori died.

Great Monologues

When Hershel starts to go into the sick area, Maggie and Rick try to stop him. Actor Scott Wilson convinces them with an impassioned speech in 403 that encapsulates Hershel's feelings about doing the best we can for each other, even in the midst of gritty survival.

Listen, dammit! You step outside, you risk your life. You take a drink of water, you risk your life. And nowadays you breathe, and you risk your life. Every moment now, you don't have a choice; the only thing you can choose is what you're risking it for. Now, I can make these people feel better and hang on a little bit longer. I can save lives. That's reason enough to risk mine. And you know that.

Scott Wilson's arc from stubborn "lord of the manor" at the farm to a realistic and idealistic mentor and leader is impressive.

RICK: *How that woman wound up, I got close to that. If I lost Carl or Judith, if I lost this place…*

HERSHEL: *Not then, Rick. Not even then. You came back. Your boy came back. You get to come back. You do.*

Hershel supports the best in Rick and reminds him that he is strong and resilient, and that life is still possible. Hershel never lets go of this concept, right up to his death.

Hershel's practical light shines as he teaches Rick how to farm. This is where Hershel lives and breathes, and his lessons on how to grow vegetables and domesticate wild pigs bring the most crucial ingredient for stability: providing food. It is the physical manifestation of hope, a structural support for Hershel's vision of settling down, making a community and starting families. It works for a while. At the beginning of Season 4, the Rickites have taken in the hapless remaining citizens of the fallen Woodbury, there is food for all, a council is formed to decide issues, and classes and a reading hour are provided for the children. (Including secret lessons in proper knifery conducted by Carol.) During this time Maggie tells Glenn that she thinks they could try to have a baby.

Their pastoral beginning is ended when they are hit with the flu and the Governor's final attack. But Hershel's lights of positive action, steadfast determination and faith will be remembered long after he is killed by the Governor. After his death, his daughters will quote him in times of desperation to keep each other calm and focused. Maggie will share the knowledge he handed down to her as she works with Deanna in Alexandria to plan their garden. Glenn will remember Hershel's messages to believe as a source of strength when he is looking for Maggie. Rick will always remember Hershel's guidance. And Carl will remember, long after Rick is gone, the taste of beans picked fresh from the garden he helped his father grow.

At the end of Season 6, we don't know whether the Rickites and Alexandria will be able to withstand the brutality of Negan. Our group has tried to make a home in a world that isn't ready to provide one. But whether in Alexandria or somewhere else, and whether it takes two, five, or ten years, eventually civilization will take hold again, and Hershel's vision will be made real.

Tyreese

Ain't nobody gotta die today.
–Tyreese, 509, "What Happened and What's Going On"

Tyreese is a man of deep feelings, from anger and anguish to nurturing and forgiveness, caught in a completely violent world. He is not a leader. He has no desire to sit on a council and make weighty decisions, nor does he want to be a warrior. He doesn't really want to be a part of the ruthlessness of this world. And ultimately, he is not.

It would be easy to apply the term "gentle giant" to Tyreese, but that would be giving short shrift to his many roles—lover, brother, protector, diplomat, and hopefully, prophet. He knows that holding onto anger blocks your growth and vision, because he went through it. He instinctively understands an important fact about forgiveness: it is not the same as absolution.

In our world, we often get these two concepts confused and mashed together. We think that forgiving someone means that the offender will never have to pay for their crimes, or that we have to be content with the consequences they receive even if we don't think the punishment is enough. "All is forgiven" means that it's over, it's done, there will be no more repercussions. But that is not forgiveness. That is absolution.

Absolution is "formal release from guilt, obligation or punishment."[1] In the Catholic Church, only priests, in their authority through Christ, can perform the ritual that remits the guilt and penalty due to a sin, and offers reconciliation with God and the Church as part of the sacrament of confession and penitence.[2] In Protestantism, people go directly to God through prayer for absolution.

So if absolution and forgiveness are separated, what does forgiveness do? To forgive is to release our own need to see or control the punishment. It is a personal, emotional decision that has little or nothing to do with any karma or consequences that the offender may receive; its purpose is only to let go of our own negative feelings about the event. To say "I forgive" is to say "I release my anger." This is what Tyreese expresses with his forgiveness.

Tyreese and his sister, Sasha, join the prison community in 316 as members of the fallen Woodbury. It is a time of calm and rebuilding, and spirits are as high as could be expected in the middle of a zombie apocalypse. Tyreese and Karen, another former Woodbury resident, fall in love after spending time together stabbing walkers in the head through the prison fence. It is a daily task for the community, but

---

1 Oxford English Dictionary online, http://www.oxforddictionaries.com/definition/english/absolution

2 https://www.catholicculture.org/culture/library/dictionary/index.cfm?id=31597

Tyreese finally tells her he doesn't want to do it anymore. "You always volunteered to do it," she says. His response is sweet. "That's because you were always doin' it. Just thought I could get to know you."

Ty is happiest with Karen in his arms, but his heart's joy doesn't last. Karen and another man are murdered; their bodies dragged into a courtyard and burned. This is the beginning of Ty's difficult journey from anger to forgiveness.

When Tyreese finds the bodies, his deep feelings turn to rage and he physically attacks both Rick and Daryl in the courtyard amid the charred remains. It is not that he thinks either are guilty; he simply loses control in his shock and anger. In 403, he yells at Rick:

> *You were a cop. You find out who did this and you bring 'em to me, you understand? You bring 'em to me!*

His rage continues as he digs graves for the two victims, attacking the ground that is yawning open. Bob suggests that he get some rest, and Tyreese responds with a flat, angry tone, "Not until they in the ground." Digging their graves is actually an act of nurturing; he is making sure they are respected, even in death. Their needs come before his own.

But Tyreese's anger also makes him self-destructive. In 404, he is with a group on a run to get antibiotics for the flu victims. Their car is blocked by a herd of walkers, and Daryl, Michonne and Bob quickly get out and

Random Thought

You gotta feel sorry for the walkers who are so decomposed that they don't have a stomach for their food to go to. One walker in a forest is nothing more than moss and skeleton rotting into a tree, and any food that it manages to munch is going to fall through its rib cage and out onto the ground. It's the walker version of bulimia.

run into the woods. But Tyreese just sits in the car. Bob has to call to him several times in desperation to get him to come out. When he finally does, he is surrounded by a mob of walkers and only his exceptional strength and trademark hammer enable him to fight through the horde.

Later, the group finds a gas station overgrown with vines, and Daryl wants to get inside to look for a car battery. Instead of being cautious, Tyreese starts hacking at the vines with brute force, heedless of any walkers that may be hidden behind the growth. When a walker does appear, Ty actually pulls it through the vines and fights with it rather than letting it go or stabbing it in the head. He ends up falling backwards and pulling the walker on top of him, forcing Daryl to pull it off and Bob to shoot it.

Michonne confronts Ty about this.

> MICHONNE: *You should have let him go.*
> TYREESE: *The hell you know about it, huh? You the damn expert?*
> MICHONNE: *No. I just don't want to see you die. Is that what you're trying to do? Do you even know what you're trying to do? I know you're pissed, and you have every reason to be. But anger makes you stupid. And stupid gets you killed.*

She recognizes an important truth that Tyreese later offers to Sasha: anger clouds your vision.

Ty still doesn't know who killed Karen and David, but Rick does. The former deputy sheriff has figured it out, asks Carol if she did it and she confesses. She says both Karen and David had the flu, and she had to try to keep it from spreading. Rick takes her on a supply run and exiles her. He wants to tell Tyreese, but before he has a chance, the Governor launches his final attack.

In the confusion, Ty ends up on the road with three very vulnerable young girls: the teenage Lizzie, her younger sister Mika, and Rick's baby, Judith. Between taking Michonne's message to heart and his need to take care of these young girls, his rage fades into the background. Rage isn't in his nature, anyway.

On the road, Carol finds them. She sees the smoke rising from the prison, ignores her own exile and drives back to find the devastating aftermath of the attack. She catches up with Tyreese and the girls, who are all delighted to see her. Lizzie has already slipped and called her Mom. The adults and three children find a charming house in the middle of a stand of pecan trees and decide to stay there. The episode at that house, 414, "The Grove," is one of *TWD*'s most heartbreaking, and the deaths of Lizzie and Mika end Carol's resistance to confessing to Ty.

Coming back from hunting for deer, Ty and Carol find a horrifying sight: Lizzie holding a bloody knife and Mika lying on the ground. Lizzie has stabbed her younger sister in an effort to prove her view that

Great Acting Moments

Brighton Sharbino does a fabulous job playing the insane Lizzie Samuels, who sees the walkers as just people who have "changed," feeds them mice, says she can hear the walkers' thoughts and ultimately kills her sister to prove that she is right. Brighton doesn't act a stereotyped concept of insane; she shows us Lizzie's complete sincerity in what she believes, and her performance in "The Grove" is wonderful. Her frantic, repetitive rant after Carol kills the walker with which she was "playing" is gripping.

You killed her! You killed her! It's the same thing! What if I killed you! What if I killed you! You don't understand, you don't understand, you don't understand, you don't understand, you don't understand! You didn't have to, you didn't have to! She didn't want to hurt anybody! She didn't want to hurt anybody! She was my friend and you killed her!

Brighton twists our heartstrings portraying a girl so insane that she doesn't understand why killing her sister was wrong. Shoulda gotta Emmy.

the walkers aren't dangerous. She is perfectly cheerful as she tells the adults, "Don't worry. She'll come back. I didn't hurt her brain."

There are no psychiatrists, no mental hospitals, and no psychotropic medicines. Lizzie is mortally dangerous, and she has already said that she can help Judith "change." Carol and Tyreese don't even dare go to sleep, leaving Lizzie unsupervised in the house. As Carol says, "She can't be with other people." So Carol takes Lizzie out to a field, telling her it is to pick some flowers for when Mika "wakes up." Crying, she tells Lizzie she loves her, and shoots her in the head.

After they have buried both girls, Carol and Tyreese sit at a card table by candlelight, in shock. Carol slowly pushes her gun across the table to Tyreese and confesses.

> *I killed Karen and David. I had to stop the illness from breaking out. I had to stop other people from dying. It wasn't Lizzie. It wasn't a stranger. Tyreese, it was me.*

Referring to the gun, she tells him to do whatever he has to do. The shock shows on Tyreese's face, and his grief and anger return. He squeezes his hand over the top of the gun. He grips the sides of the table as if his life depended on it. He asks Carol if Karen suffered or if she was scared, and Carol answers no.

Tyreese slowly pushes the gun aside. He speaks in a tense whisper.

> *I forgive you. I'm never gonna forget. It happened. You did it. You feel it. I know you do. It's a part of you now. Me, too. But, I forgive you.*

How could Tyreese so easily forgive the murder of the woman he loved? It gets back to the difference between forgiveness and absolution. Tyreese is not offering absolution; he is only releasing his need to control or see the punishment. He has been through the rage and knows how damaging it is. He knows that Carol is a good person who feels remorse for her action, and that she will pay for it all of her life in her own heart.

In 509, as he is dying, the spirit of the Governor confronts him about forgiving Carol, and Tyreese has to defend his decision. He tells the Governor, "I forgave her, because it isn't over."

It is this line that shows he is separating forgiveness and absolution. It isn't over. The world is still awful, and she has to live in it. There may be karmic payment she needs to make in the future, but he doesn't need to be there or even know about it. It is hers to experience. It also isn't over because she still has opportunities to learn, people to protect, and ways to make up for her mistakes with Karen and David. These will all happen without him being there to control it.

Forgiving in these terms takes trust. Whether you trust in a Divine creator, karma, or simply the natural order of the universe, it takes trust that there will be consequences, and humility to let go of the ego that thinks you know what the consequences should be. It takes knowing that the scales of the universe will always be balanced, karma is inevitable, and we can let God (or Yahweh or Shiva or Allah) handle it. According to reincarnation, even if the person never has consequences in this life, they will happen in another life. The nature of those depends on how truly contrite the person is. The Bible says, "Vengeance is mine, sayeth the Lord." To me, the emphasis is not on *vengeance*; it is on *mine*. Only God (or Yahweh or Shiva or Allah) truly knows what is in a person's heart, and is best equipped to give out the appropriate response.

So what is the benefit to Tyreese of giving up his need to see Carol punished? Releasing his anger is the emotional win. That is what rolls the stone off of his heart. Anger is a solid wall that blocks our connection with others—even those who we love. Tyreese's forgiveness heals his relationship with Carol. He is essentially saying, "You may have more debt to pay, but when or how that happens isn't up to me, and I don't want my anger to get in the way of our relationship." Tyreese is a man who wants connection with others, so he is willing to let go.

As a bearer of light, Tyreese will pass along any wisdom he learns. He does this for Sasha, who is going through her own rage after the Terminians eat Bob's leg. As Bob lays dying in 503, she chooses to leave his side to join the warriors in the plan to attack the Terminians. Ty tries to talk her out of it.

TYREESE: *I know how it feels. But this right here, the time you could have with him, you can't throw that away. I wish I had it with Karen.*
SASHA: *Do you remember how you felt? What you wanted to do?*
TYREESE: *Yeah. It made it so I couldn't see it. Forgiveness. That's facing it.*
SASHA: *I should forgive them? For hurting him? For trying to kill us? What the hell is wrong with you? You think we have a choice?*
TYREESE: *Not all of us. Just you. When he opens his eyes, the only thing he's gonna want to see is your face.*

Sasha is mixing together absolution and forgiveness. For her, to let go of her anger means that there will be no justice; the consequences will somehow be erased. She wants consequences; she wants to see them and be part of enforcing them. She goes with the warriors, and she does help kill the last of the cannibals. (In this case, consequences were necessary because the threat was still active. But Ty was right—she herself didn't need to be there. Another Rickite would have understood if she wanted to stay with Bob, and would have gone with the warriors in her stead.)

Bob holds on long enough to have his last moments with Sasha after the attack. Only after he dies does she let go a little, allowing her brother to act as her proxy to stab Bob in the head. But this just makes her angry again—this time at herself—for not being strong enough. In 507, "Crossed," Tyreese again shines his light for her.

SASHA: *I should've been able to do it myself.*
TYREESE: *You could've. But you let yourself feel it. You kept your eyes open. You let me help you.*

Here are three important notes. Forgiving and releasing anger doesn't mean being a doormat. Criminal and abusive acts must be stopped. When a crime happens in our world we should do everything within the legal system to ensure that consequences are enforced. In relationships, no one should accept abusive behavior because they trust that there will be consequences for the person at some point in time that they don't have to see. If hurt is continuing to be inflicted, that must end,

Random Thought

It is Carl who establishes the unspoken rule that the head stab should be done by the person who is emotionally the closest to the person who died. In 304, "The Killer Within," after his mother has died, it is Carl who shoots her in the head. In 610, "The Next World," Spencer goes into the woods to search for his walker-mother, Deanna. When Carl finds her instead, he uses himself as bait to lead her to Spencer so that Spencer can end her un-dead, un-life. Michonne confronts Carl about risking his own life, and Carl makes the rule public.

> MICHONNE: *You could have killed her.*
> CARL: *No, I couldn't! I wouldn't!*
> MICHONNE: *Was this some sort of game out there? Did you think that…*
> CARL: *No!*
> MICHONNE: *Then why?*
> CARL: *Because it should be someone who loved her! Someone who's family! And I, I'd do it for you.*

It is a lovely moment for two reasons. First, because what Carl has said is emotionally true—it is best for someone who loves the person to do this. If that's not possible, a chosen proxy would still be better than a stranger. Second, because Carl has spoken his feelings about Michonne—she is family. And soon enough this family unit will be fully established when Rick and Michonne kiss and spend their first night together.

whether by stopping the behavior or by leaving the relationship. But once the offender has been stopped or the relationship has been ended, we can work on releasing the anger.

Second, offenses that are more serious or ongoing, and offenders who don't express any remorse, will present a bigger challenge to forgiving, naturally. Many criminals are either never caught or never repentant, or we may experience hurt from someone we love who never does understand their actions. It takes great effort to forgive in these situations, but it helps to understand that forgiveness is not the same as absolution.

Finally, working through anger and pain doesn't mean the memory or hurt will be completely eliminated. Some experiences are nearly impossible to get over completely. But the pain and anger can move into the background and become part of the fabric of life. Even if it takes months or years, working through and releasing the pain and anger and reminding ourselves to trust that the offender will undergo exactly the right consequences, whether in this life or the next, will eventually lessen the weight of these negative emotions. As Michonne tells Father Gabriel in 503 when he confides in her that he hears the screams of his parishioners in his nightmares, "Yeah. That won't stop. But it won't be all the time."

Tyreese dreams of Karen, too, and of seeing someone kill her. We don't know whether those dreams became less frequent after he moved from rage to forgiveness. Hopefully so.

Tyreese's nonviolent nature plays a role when the Rickites learn that Beth and Carol are being held captive at Grady Memorial Hospital. They plan a rescue, and Rick outlines a full attack. Tyreese offers the less violent option of taking two guards captive and proposing a prisoner exchange. Rick is doubtful, but Daryl supports Tyreese and they move forward with his plan. It doesn't work perfectly. Three people are killed, but only because the leader at the hospital, Dawn, scuttles the deal by making an additional demand at the last minute. It is not Tyreese's fault.

They live in a world that requires violence for survival, and Tyreese continually struggles with this reality. Even in 501, when he saves Judith from the Terminian Martin with repeated pummeling of Martin's head, he roars his pain, "I won't! I won't! I won't!" with each blow. In the end, he is true to his word. He doesn't kill Martin. His beatings leave Martin unconscious, and Martin lives on to be part of the group that consumes Bob's leg.

In 509, Tyreese is called upon to defend his forgiving and nonviolent nature, and is offered the choice to stay in this world or leave.

In what is the most purely spiritual episode of the series so far, the Rickites drive to Noah's subdivision to find his family. No one is left alive in Noah's former neighborhood. Most of the Rickites go scavenging, and Tyreese goes with Noah to his house.

Noah's mother is dead and his younger brothers are walkers. One of them bites Tyreese on the arm, and Noah runs to get help. Alone in the house, losing blood and dying, Tyreese is visited by the spirits of several people he knew in life, all bearing the wounds that killed them. A clock radio has stopped, yet the voices of reporters drone on describing war atrocities and other timeless violence.

Great Writing

In 501, after the group is reunited and they look at the black smoke rising over Terminus, we have this exchange between Rick and Carol:

RICK: *I don't know if the fire's still burning.*
CAROL: *It is.*

The words are insignificant to the rest of the group, and Rick's only response is that they should get going. But it was Mika who told Carol in 414 that when smoke is black, the fire is still burning. At the time, Mika smiled and said in her innocence, "I miss science class." When we hear Carol's comment, we remember, along with her, two small bodies buried in the grove, and our hearts give a small, sad sigh. *TWD* is full of these moments; sometimes tender, sometimes angry. Writing shoulda gotta Emmy.

Great Monologues

Chad Coleman's monologue as Tyreese dies is one of the very best of the show. Tyreese has crawled underneath a child's desk, but when the Governor condemns his forgiveness, he forces himself to stand and face the psychopathic leader. He points his finger accusingly, and his anger and tears come through.

I said I would do what I had to to earn my keep, but I didn't know you. But I know, I know who I am. I know what happened and what's going on. I know. You didn't show me shit. You, you're dead. Everything that you were is dead, and it's, it's not over. I forgave her because it's not over. It's not over. It's, it's not over. I didn't turn away. I kept listening to the news so I could do what I could to help! I'm not givin' up, you hear me? I'm not giving up! People like me, people like me, they can live. Ain't nobody gotta die today.

Absolutely gorgeous. Shoulda gotta Emmy. Really.

Martin, who Tyreese did not kill, criticizes the nonviolence. He says that if Tyreese had killed him, then perhaps Bob wouldn't have been killed, perhaps having Bob alive could have saved Beth, and perhaps Ty wouldn't have been bitten now. "Domino shit."

Bob joins the spirits and says that's ridiculous. "I got bit at the food bank. It went the way it had to. The way it was always going to. Just like this."

Mika and Lizzie appear and tell Tyreese, "It's better now."

Beth appears with a guitar and sings, and tells him, "It's okay, Tyreese. You gotta know that now."

Bob tells him, "It's okay that you didn't want to be a part of it anymore, Ty." They assure him that if he wants to surrender to his own death and move on from the violence, it is okay.

Then the Governor appears and challenges him. Tyreese had been part of Woodbury briefly, and the Governor now berates Tyreese for not adapting to the violence. He ridicules Tyreese's forgiveness, almost spitting out the words with disgust, "That you would sit there in front of a woman who killed someone you loved, and you would forgive her."

Ty has defended his choices beautifully. After he has completed this task and collapses (with a push by the spirit-Governor) onto the floor, his friends run into the room. Rick shouts orders, Michonne uses her katana to amputate his arm above the bite, and they support him, half-conscious and half-walking, out of the house and down the street. They sit a fading Tyreese on the pavement as they fight off a small crowd of walkers at the subdivision entrance, and lead him through the forest. Beth sings in the background and Bob says again, "It went the way it had to. The way it was always going to." Firmly in this world, Rick insists to Ty, "You gotta hold on, man. Hold on!" Finally, Ty is unable to walk at all, and his four friends run through the forest, carrying him to their van.

After they lay him in the back seat, Rick, Michonne, Glenn and Noah are replaced by Bob, Beth, Lizzie and Mika. Ty stood up for his beliefs, stood up for forgiveness, and stood firm with the idea that people who work for nonviolence have a place in this world; Martin and the Governor are no longer there.

The otherworldly radio news tells of cannibalism in refugee camps, destruction of entire villages and mutilation of mothers and children. Tyreese has had enough violence. He stares out the window, tears streaming, and speaks his last.

> TYREESE: *Turn it off.*
> BOB: *You sure?*
> BETH: *It's okay Tyreese. You gotta know that now.*
> LIZZIE: *It isn't just okay.*
> MIKA: *It's better now.*

Tyreese lays his head against the window and watches the trees going by outside. With his hold on this life slipping away, they slowly fade into a blurry grey, and then into black.

Tyreese was wrong. He did die that day. The violence of their world (and ours) is far from over. But what if everyone took Tyreese's advice? What if everyone, instead of holding tight onto anger, fear and resentment that was built up over years (and sometimes over multiple lives, I believe), worked through these negatives emotions and experiences and let them go? What if all children were taught how to express their negative feelings constructively and honestly, and we all grew up knowing how to do that? It might take a few generations, but then perhaps Tyreese's role as a prophet would be made real. At least in terms of violence, "Ain't nobody gotta die today."

The Deer

There's still a life for us, a place, maybe like this. It isn't all death out there.
–Rick to Lori, 202, "Save the Last One"

In 201, Rick, Shane, and Carl are looking for Sophia in a forest after they have left a church, and they spot a deer through the trees. It is a beautiful animal, lit in fresh, soft, dappled sunlight. It is nibbling leaves in a clearing in front of them, unafraid. It looks at them casually and flicks its ears, and Carl is entranced. They have been through so much horror, but in this quiet moment in the forest, Carl is just a normal ten-year-old boy, in awe at how close he is to this large wild animal.

Rick nods, encouraging him to quietly approach the deer. The deer looks right at Carl, and Carl takes one slow, cautious step, then another, then another. He is just a few yards away when the gunshot rings out. The bullet goes right through the deer and into Carl. He falls and the horrified hunter, Otis, comes out of the brush. He did not see Carl, and tells Rick and Shane to take Carl to the farm where he works.

Rick runs more than a half mile carrying Carl. When they reach the farmhouse, Hershel begins work, giving directions to his daughters and Otis' wife, Patricia. They gather towels and instruments, working with speed and efficiency. Hershel extracts one bullet fragment, but there are more that are deeper.

After Hershel's daughter Maggie finds Lori and brings her to the farm, Hershel tells the parents that Carl is bleeding internally from a nicked artery and that he will die if Hershel doesn't go in to close it up—but he has no respirator to help Carl breath while under the anesthesia. Hershel can do the surgery without the respirator, but it is very unlikely that Carl will survive it.

Shane and Otis leave to find a respirator at a nearby FEMA shelter. As the hours go by and they don't return, Carl's condition deteriorates. Hershel tells Rick and Lori that if he doesn't begin soon, Carl will die.

Great Monologues

Actress Sarah Wayne Callies gives us one of the best monologues in 304, when Lori goes into labor while trapped in the prison boiler room with Carl and Maggie. She knows she will need a C-section, and that it will kill her. She begs Maggie to save her baby, and she is intense and strong and loving and tearful as she says goodbye to Carl.

> *You are gonna be fine. You are gonna beat this world, I know you will. You are smart, and you are strong, and you are so brave, and I love you... You promise me you'll always do what's right. It's so easy to do the wrong thing in this world. So, so if it feels wrong, don't do it, alright? If it feels easy, don't do it, don't let the world spoil you. You're so good. My sweet boy, you're the best thing I ever did. I love you. I love you. My sweet, sweet boy, I love you. Okay. Okay, now.*

She looks at the ceiling, lets out a small breath, and whispers to the absent Rick, "Goodnight, Love." Then she screams as Maggie cuts the knife across her stomach. Again, shoulda gotta Emmy.

Rick and Lori are alone on Hershel's front porch, and Lori suggests that perhaps letting Carl go would be for the best. If he dies, he would be spared any more of their nightmare life; he would have no more running, starving, and being afraid of being caught by a walker. She asks Rick why it would be better for Carl to live. Rick is horrified by the question, but he doesn't have an answer for her.

Later that night, Carl wakes up and sees his mother for the first time since he was shot. He tells her that he hurts. But then his young face lights with a smile, and he tells her about his experience.

> CARL: *You should have seen it.*
> LORI: *What?*
> CARL: *The deer. It was so pretty, Mom. It was so close. I've never been…*

With his blood abandoning its normal arterial pathways, his brain is not getting enough oxygen and he starts convulsing. Hershel tells Rick and Lori that they have to decide soon, and now Rick has the answer to Lori's question. He knows why, even in an apocalypse, it is better to hope.

> *That's what he was talking about when he woke up. Not about gettin' shot, or what happened at the church. He talked about something beautiful, something living…It isn't all death out there; it can't be. We just have to be strong enough after everything we've seen to still believe that. Why is it better for Carl to live, even in this world? He talked about the deer, Lori. He talked about the deer.*

The deer gave Carl a moment to hold onto. It reached him, made him forget all the horror and lifted him up beyond the awfulness of the past weeks, and it was the first thing he wanted to tell his mother. And that story, in turn, gave Rick the answer he needed to convince Lori to keep trying, to reach for the highest and best option even when everything seemed hopeless.

Most of us have gone through our own times of hopeless despair. Whether it is divorce, the death of someone we love, job loss, abuse, or addiction, we can go through our own small, personal apocalypse.

But no matter how black things seem, we do not know what the future holds. There is always reason to hope. And if we are open to them, we can receive the light messages that help us to hold on during the dark times.

The bearers of light that cross our paths are not always human. It is up to us to recognize and appreciate them, and let them work their wonder on us. Carl did. He talked about the deer.

2

Religion Does
Not Equal Faith

I still think there's a plan. I still believe there's a reason.
–Hershel, 405, "Internment"

I'm a sinner. I sin almost every day. But those sins, I confess them to God.
Not strangers.
–Father Gabriel, 502, "Strangers"

The two main faith figures in *TWD* are Hershel and Father Gabriel Stokes, and they could not be more different. Hershel, the farmer and veterinarian, is a Christian who reads the Bible and knows it well. But his faith goes beyond religion. It is a deep part of him, and requires no church, preacher, or outer trappings to survive. Father Gabriel, the Episcopal priest and alleged religious professional, has no inner faith. When we meet him, he lives in fear, shrinking away from trust and life.

The other faith figures in the show are Rick, Maggie and Daryl (yes, Daryl). Their spiritual roles are not as obvious, but they do bring out important thoughts on faith.

Hershel: *Faith Beyond the Text*

Hershel's faith is internalized, deeper than mere proclamations of rules and regulations and belief in miracles performed long ago. Hershel sees miracles in current life events; he sees God in the land and all around him. His faith supports him, regardless of outer circumstances or whether he has access to external religious trappings. It is this inner faith that helps him maintain his positive point of view through the end of the known world.

If the topic comes up, Hershel will state his own beliefs proudly. But he also respects the beliefs of others and sees no need to push his theology. In 204, "Cherokee Rose," he shows Rick a view overlooking a beautiful valley. He tells Rick that it's good to pause and reflect and that his own thoughts turn to God in those moments. He asks Rick for his thoughts on the matter, and when Rick expresses his spiritual cynicism, Hershel presses only briefly.

> HERSHEL: *Lori told me your story. How you were shot, your coma. Yet you came out of it somehow. You did not feel God's hand in yours?*
> RICK: *In that moment, no I did not.*

Rick tells Hershel, "I try not to mix it up with the Almighty anymore," and once Rick states his case, Hershel drops the issue. He sees Rick as a grown man who can make his own decisions and who will or won't move along a faith path regardless of anything Hershel says. He leaves Rick's relationship with God to Rick and God. And he trusts that if the Almighty wants to provide Rick with experiences that will open him to spirituality, then the Almighty is more than capable of doing so without Hershel sticking his nose into the matter.

When the "Asian boy," Glenn, falls in love with Maggie, Hershel never asks Glenn about his religion. Not once. He sees that Maggie loves Glenn, and that Glenn is an honest man who is brave and smart and has saved Maggie's life. He trusts in the words of the Savior in whom he believes, that God knows what is in a person's heart, and it is God's place to judge, not his.

Ironically, not pushing your faith onto others is in itself a sign of faith. It is not possible to preach your way into a heart that isn't ready, and continuing to press the subject is a sign of nothing more than a need to control. The impulse to judge and reject is only ego expressing anger and fear. It also blocks light from flowing through, and Hershel is wiser than that. He knows that letting people see his light is the best way to draw someone to faith, if they are open to it at all. And even then, he doesn't get attached to the hope of converting anybody. He lets them be. That is trust.

How do we attain an internal faith such as Hershel's? One important ingredient is to let go of the need for proof. Not just proof of a Divine being, but proof that there will be a happy ending to the challenges we face in life. Hershel doesn't need to see the resolution of any situation in order to trust that ultimately, it will be alright because there is a purpose. Even after the flu epidemic demolishes the community they worked so hard to establish, Hershel tells Rick, "I still believe there's a plan. I still believe there's a reason."

This is not blind faith or fatalism. It is a faith that looks forward. It is adjusting our attitude and actions as if the end of the story is good, even if we are living in the middle with the toughest times. It is continuing to trust this principle even if death comes, as it did for Hershel, before the purpose is revealed or the tough times get easier. It is the humility to accept that we don't have all the answers. Believing this way doesn't make painful events any less difficult, but it does help us get through them without getting buried in self-pity or anger.

Letting go of the need to know the end of our story, our family's story, or our society's story, helps to release negative emotions like anger, resentment and grief. And that is the true goal. I believe that for all of us, the ultimate purpose of life is our learning and growth, letting go of clinging emotions, and removing the obstacles that block the connection between our inner Divine Spark and the Outer Divine.

Loosening the control that fear, jealousy and anger have on us is precisely how a person can follow the instructions of the Bible's Matthew 7:5, to "take the log out of your own eye." I believe this is how we find Heaven on Earth, because as we make step-by-step progress in removing the log (negative emotions), we clear our connection to the Divine. We see and hear more clearly and positively. And the great thing is, this can be done by any human being, anytime, anywhere, regardless of what religion or denomination that person holds, or even if they have no religion at all. It is simply a function of our energy, part of the anatomy of our soul. Different religions have different ways to instruct us on this, but the goal and the effect are the same.

Another good thing about Hershel's faith is that it is a living faith. His focus is on a relationship with God and how we treat other people, not just quoting text. Getting bogged down in the text of written scripture can make faith become petrified and fossilized. There is great value in sacred texts, and certainly Hershel himself knows the Bible well and comes back to it time after time. But scripture from any tradition can be a reminder of great wisdom, or it can be a trap for the ego. I haven't read all the world's sacred books, but if other texts are like the Bible, they contain spiritual truths as well as verses that people can use to support their own fear and anger and block the light between themselves and others.

In addition, there are faith traditions around the world that use no written scriptures, but operate on ritual and oral traditions only. People within those traditions are just as spiritual (or not) as people who go by sacred text. There is wisdom in stories told and rituals enacted, and these practices can aid in removing negative emotional concrete and improving the Divine connection.

Fighting over the names for God also blocks the Divine flow. People around the world have different names for the Divine: God, Yahweh, Allah, Great Spirit, Grandmother, Shiva, Vishnu, Demeter, Kwan Yin, Olorun, Eshu, and on and on. When you include localized beliefs and polytheistic traditions such as Hinduism, the list multiplies exponentially. But often, we humans decide what to think of someone based on the name they use for God, or we say their God is a "false" god. It's ridiculous. How we treat each other matters, but someone else's name for God doesn't matter one whit.

Think of it this way. If God is a Tree, I may look at the Tree and call it a Boogaloo Tree. You may call it a Hot Diggity Tree. Someone else may call it a Rama Lama Tree. But none of this changes the Tree in any way. The Tree stays the same. The Tree bears the same flowers, leaves, and seeds, and it has the same hardness or softness of wood and pattern of bark, no matter what we call it. And the Tree looks down on our fussing and fighting and tries to tell us, "Hey. Guys. Cut it out, will ya? I've got shade over here, you can have a picnic under Me, and I'm happy for you to tie a rope swing onto one of My branches and the kids can have fun."

Unfortunately, if our faith is stuck and fossilized, we will then start fighting over whether the Tree is a provider of shade, a place to break bread, or a way for our children to play. (Then the Tree says, "Guys. Really. Get out of the sun—it's baking your brains.") The Tree doesn't change, no matter how much we argue. So what can change? Only us. We can change in the level of fullness in how we view the Tree.

Here is another way to think about it. Imagine that God is living in Kansas. Saying that there is only one true path to God is like saying the only way to get to Kansas is from Oregon. But this is far from true. You can get to Kansas from Oregon, California, Florida, Maine, or anywhere else in the United States. You can get to Kansas from France, Uruguay or Thailand. You can get to Kansas from anywhere, as long as you take the trip. It may not be a straight path—you may run out of gas, take a wrong turn, or just decide to do a little sightseeing (though too much sightseeing can be an indication that you aren't taking your destination seriously). As long as you follow your chosen path with faith and steadfastness, you will get to Kansas.

Reincarnation says that we experience lives in a variety of religious traditions: shamanistic, indigenous, western, eastern, modern, ancient, monotheistic, pantheistic, polytheistic, or atheistic. We take many paths on our way to opening to our Divine connection. Each path has its value, and each serves a purpose.

What does all of this have to do with Hershel? We have no indication from *TWD* that Hershel believed in reincarnation, but he does show his belief that everyone has to find their own way, and that everyone has light to shine, regardless of their religious background.

Hershel's faith also allows him to face his death with calm and bravery. (Not that there's anything wrong with fear or anger in the face of a violent, sudden death. That's just being human.) He dies in 408 during the final attack on the prison. After being kidnapped by the Governor, he is on his knees as the Governor demands that Rick turn over the prison. Throughout this interchange, Hershel's focus is not on the Governor nor on the sword at his neck, and the look on his face is not one of fear. He watches Rick with a small smile of pride as Rick tries to convince the Governor that the two groups can live in the prison in different cell blocks, get to know each other slowly, and put the past behind them.

It's not that Hershel wants to be a martyr. He speaks up to the man who has his life in his hands and supports Rick's ideas. "It could work. You know it could."

But though Rick tells the Governor, "We can all come back," his hopeful and life-affirming words fall on deaf ears. The Governor whispers one word, "Liar," and Hershel dies when the Governor decapitates him with the sword. Hershel never begged, he never pleaded, he never resented, he never feared. It wasn't the hardened bravery of a soldier. It was simple faith and not clinging to anything, including his own life.

Hershel shows us the best of Christianity and other organized religions—his faith goes deeper than written scripture and doesn't get petrified in dogma. He believes in rules, structure, and tradition, but the rules don't rule him. He knows he is not perfect and he doesn't judge others. He simply believes in the existence of Divinity, is humble before the Author of the story of his life, and holds hands in prayer with his daughters as trouble looms outside the prison. He respects the Bible and worships God. Not the other way around.

Father Gabriel: *The Pathway Through the Dark*

Hershel's belief finds its opposite in Father Gabriel, whose faith is no deeper than the cardboard collar around his neck and whose fear is deep and abiding. Father Gabriel wants to know God; he wouldn't have become a priest if he didn't. But his flimsy faith in the Divine requires crutches—a collar, a church, a congregation. It has not yet been internalized. If Hershel and Father Gabriel had ever met, it would be Hershel teaching Father Gabriel about God, not the other way around. As Hershel's spiritual heir, his daughter Maggie plays a significant role with the cowardly, guilt-ridden priest.

After months of living alone in St. Sarah's Episcopal Church in the nightmare of the zombie apocalypse, Father Gabriel's true horror begins after meeting Rick's group. He knows this himself. He has committed atrocities through inaction, and he tells Rick, "The Lord sent you to punish me." The Rickites hold up a mirror and force him to look. They rip away the outer shell of his hypocrisy, lay bare the shrinking, betraying, self-serving soul inside and start him on a path that almost tears him apart. He goes through self-hate—but hating yourself for something you've done is not the same as an honest sense of guilt and remorse. Self-hate for crimes and misdemeanors can be self-destructive, and is never the true end of the path. Accepting yourself (including what you did), reforming both your attitude and actions and living a new life is.

At the end of Season 6, Father Gabriel appears to have come through this storm. If this change is real and it lasts, it will be one of the most meaningful stories of growth of any character in the show. But before Father Gabriel can find the light, the descent into his own personal hell happens in phases.

Phase 1: The Confessional

In 502, the Rickites are on the road after their near escape from Terminus when they hear Father Gabriel's screams for help and find him huddled on top of a large rock, unable to deal with the small handful of walkers reaching up for him. The Rickites easily dispatch the walkers, and Rick asks Father Gabriel the three questions: How many walkers have you killed? How many people have you killed? Why?

Father Gabriel says he hasn't killed any walkers, and his helplessness with them is clear. However, he also claims he hasn't killed any humans. Why? "Because the Lord abhors violence." This statement of innocence doesn't sit well with our experienced crew, who know that anyone who has survived this long has committed acts they would never have imagined in the civilized world.

Father Gabriel leads Rick's group to his church, and Rick's suspicion is heightened when Carl finds the words, "You will burn for this" scratched into one of the outside walls. Rick again confronts Gabriel, telling him it is obvious that he is hiding something and letting him know, "That's your business. But these people...these people are my family. And if what you're hiding somehow hurts them in any way, I'll kill you."

Great Monologues

Seth Gilliam's "I always lock the doors at night" speech in 503 is amazing. His confusion and fear as Rick pushes him, then his anguish as he tells how he killed his congregation are all beautifully done.

I lock the doors at night. I always lock the doors at night, I always lock the doors at night. They started coming, my congregation. Atlanta was bombed the night before and they were scared. They were, they were looking for a safe place, a place where they felt safe. And it was so early, it was so early. And the doors were still locked. You see, it was my choice. There were so many of them, and they were trying to pry the shutters, and banging on the sidings, screaming at me, and so the dead came for them. Women. Children. Entire families calling my name as they were torn apart.

Seth brings us a man whose world is starting to crumble, and who has to build it back up again, emotional brick by emotional brick.

Unfortunately for Father Gabriel, this is exactly what appears to happen. Daryl and Carol go missing, and Bob is kidnapped by the remaining Terminians, who cut off his lower leg, roast it over a fire, and eat it in front of him.

The Rickites believe that Father Gabriel is connected to these incidents, and in 503, Rick flatly accuses him of it. Father Gabriel insists it isn't true, but Rick will no longer put up with the priest's claims of purity and demands answers:

'You'll burn for this'? That was for you. Why? What are you going to burn for, Gabriel? What? What did you do?! What did you do?!

As Rick grabs his jacket, Father Gabriel finally breaks down and confesses that he kept his congregation locked out of the church, doing nothing as they were devoured by the walkers. He sobs and sinks to the floor. Contrary to his claims, he has killed. And even though he has technically confessed, he isn't ready yet to take full responsibility.

Why did Father Gabriel refuse to open the doors for his congregants? It makes no sense—more people would provide more help and safety. Was he afraid that walkers would have gotten into the church? Possibly, but he could have looked out a window and seen whether there were any walkers nearby. If there had been walkers close to the church, his congregation wouldn't have approached in the first place. Father Gabriel says it himself, "…and so the dead came for them." The dead came only after his parishioners started yelling. There would have been time to open the doors at least for the first arrivals.

Was he afraid of having to be a leader in a crisis situation? Possibly. (Only Seth Gilliam knows for sure.) He said, "There were so many," and he was talking about his congregation, not walkers. He could not face being responsible for them.

Does the canned food play a role? This is a fairly cynical point, but there was a canned food drive just before the apocalypse, and the cans are still at the church. They would last a long time for one person, not so much for a congregation. Not only does Father Gabriel not have faith in God, he has no faith in his church community or the capabilities of its members. People in groups could go on runs for supplies, protecting each other. That would have been possible, but Father Gabriel did not have that vision.

In the final analysis, he probably didn't think through any of this. He probably just woke up, heard the knocking and yelling, and thought on some primal level, "I can't." He was petrified. The word *petrified* means both "extreme fright" and "turned to stone." Petrified wood is wood that has turned to stone, and this is exactly what happened to Father Gabriel. His extreme fright turned his heart to stone and rendered him unable to move. It is the exact opposite of faith, and of Hershel's example.

Later in the episode, Rick, Michonne, Abraham and Sasha kill the remaining Terminus cannibals inside Saint Sarah's. Father Gabriel looks in horror at the carnage, at the bodies and the blood in front of the altar, and says plaintively, "This is the Lord's house." Maggie's reply is simple. "No. It's just four walls and a roof."

What Father Gabriel doesn't realize yet is that St. Sarah's Episcopal Church lost any divine purpose or connection on the morning that he bowed down to his fear and kept his parishioners locked out. The Lord's house became four walls and a roof weeks ago, and Rick and his group had nothing to do with it.

Phase II: Holding Up the Mirror

Despite revealing his failings (or maybe because he finally did), the Rickites bring Father Gabriel with them when they leave the church and head from Atlanta to Virginia to try to get Noah back home. Beth has been killed, and when they get to Noah's subdivision, Tyreese dies there.

They decide to press on to DC, but their vehicles soon run out of gas. They are reduced to walking to DC, emotionally traumatized, physically weak, starving and dehydrated.

Maggie has been despondent since Beth's death. Father Gabriel walks with her in 510, "Them," and tries to play preacher; ready to listen if she wants to talk about her father or Beth. She will have none of it.

MAGGIE: *You never even met them.*

FATHER GABRIEL: *I know you're in pain.*

MAGGIE: *You don't know shit. You had a job. You were there to save your flock, right? But you didn't. You hid. Don't act like that didn't happen.*

Her father's daughter, Maggie has no desire to receive solace from a hypocrite who abandoned his post. Father Gabriel's body is starving and exhausted and his ego has been challenged directly. The Rickites see through him and he has nothing to do except walk and reflect on the man in the mirror.

The first sign that he is beginning to admit his own unworthiness to stand on any religious pedestal happens as the group takes a brief rest on the side of the road and is threatened by a pack of dogs. These animals still have collars from a time when they were pets who were fed, walked, played with and loved. But with their owners dead (or undead), they forage on their own, hungry and dangerous. With no hesitation, Sasha shoots them. Rick breaks branches into sticks, and a moment later the starving group is roasting meat. This food is a miracle, and Father Gabriel takes a reluctant bite. It is still difficult for him to accept the world as it is—he would rather hide. But he does eat, and as he chews, he removes his priest's collar and puts it into the fire; it is a good sign that he is letting go of his trappings of ego. Significantly, Maggie is the one member of the group who sees this small but significant act.

Another miracle happens when the dehydrated group is blessed with rain. They laugh, lift their faces with open mouths to catch the drops, and fall onto their backs to let the rain soak them. Father Gabriel looks up to the sky, and says simply, "I'm sorry, my Lord. I'm sorry." It is also a good sign, although we don't know what he is sorry for. For killing his flock? For eating the dogs? For not having faith?

The good news is that Father Gabriel is a self-reflective person. He could have heard Maggie's objections, decided she was full of crap and put up walls, but he didn't. And now he is firmly on a path that will lead him through deep valleys of confusion. No one has a straight road to healing wounds or dismantling the armor of ego, and Father Gabriel's journey has just begun.

Phase III: Self-Loathing Can't Be the Final Answer

If a person has done something harmful and feels no guilt, then they are either in denial, rationalizing or minimizing the hurt they caused, or are possibly a sociopath or a psychopath. Moving out of denial or rationalization into feelings of sincere guilt is a positive step. Guilt is part of our emotional anatomy. Like anger, it can serve a good purpose and be worked through, or it can become stagnant and fester inside. It can become a field of quicksand that will swallow us if we don't deal with it—especially if it grows to the level of self-hate.

Self-hate can be a dangerous no-man's land between denial and true growth; a place where we can get caught and spend a very long and sad time. It isn't the final stage in taking full responsibility. We can't fully move on and recover while in a state of self-hatred.

The true goal includes accepting our mistakes as part of our history, changing our outlook, changing our ways, and moving on. That is repentance. We think of repentance as being sorry for what we did, but the full meaning is more than that. It includes changing our point of view and turning away from the past hurtful behavior or attitudes. It is only with this that healing happens, when the sun can shine on our souls again.

Until then, it's hard to handle the feelings we have while we are lost in the mire and muck of self-hatred. So we sometimes find destructive ways to hide from them. We can try to make them go away by punishing ourselves, or avoid them by drowning in a bottle of gin, taking drugs, or indulging in other addictive and escapist actions. Or we can push them away by judging others for what we see as similar behavior.

Father Gabriel experiences the dark, dank cave of self-hate when the Rickites join the community of Alexandria. The Alexandrians have put up corrugated steel panel walls around the entire community, and they live in $800,000 houses with running water and electricity provided by a solar array. Due to a large nearby gravel pit that acts as a walker trap, they have not experienced any large-scale walker invasions. Their lives have been simplified, but not traumatized.

The Alexandrians know nothing of Father Gabriel's history, and they set up a small sanctuary in a garage where he can hold services. The first time he enters this makeshift church he discovers a basket of strawberries with a note: "We are so blessed to have you here. Rosemary." But Father Gabriel no longer sees himself as a blessing. On the lectern sits an open Bible, and after reading the note he starts tearing pages out of it, first slowly and then more rapidly. This is an expression of his self-loathing—he no longer sees himself as having any relationship to the Bible. But on another symbolic level, it is yet another a good sign.

This tearing of Bible pages is the direct opposite of a scene at St. Sarah's. As the Rickites first enter and search for walkers, Carol finds multiple Bibles laid open on the desk in Father Gabriel's office. He is starting to transcribe the Bible onto blank sheets of paper. This self-appointed Bible copying is possibly a distraction, a way to put his own misdeeds out of his mind. Or it could be an attempt at atonement. In either case, now in Alexandria, his relationship to the Bible is being torn asunder. The Bible, along with his ego identity as "pastor," can no longer hold up his faith. Again, this is not a criticism of the Bible. It is only an acknowledgement that we bring to the text as much as the text brings to us. Father Gabriel must discover a new relationship to the text. In the meantime, his faith has to find a way to stand on its own.

Father Gabriel is not conscious of this, of course. In the dark shadow of self-loathing, he tries several methods to get away from that feeling, none of which work.

First he tries projecting his bad behavior onto others and accuses the Rickites of what he sees as similar crimes. He goes to the house of Alexandria's leader, Deanna, and tells her that "Satan disguises himself," and "they are not to be trusted; they have done horrendous things. They don't deserve to be here." He is willing to have the Rickites exiled back into the walker-filled wilderness so he can get rid of the mirror and start fresh with the innocent Alexandrians.

Fortunately, Deanna is an experienced leader who doesn't automatically believe what she hears. She simply thanks Father Gabriel and tells him she has a lot to think about. (Also, in her appropriate place in Father Gabriel's story, Maggie is around the corner and hears his betrayal.)

Unable to sway the Alexandrian matriarch and lost in a semi-delirium of despair, Father Gabriel's next response is to attempt suicide-by-walker. In a daze in 516, he walks past Deanna's son, Spencer, who is guarding the Alexandria gate. He walks through the woods, comes to a road and is mere feet away from a walker who is chomping on a still-living man lying on the pavement. Father Gabriel offers himself up, holding out his arms and calling to the walker, "I'm ready." The walker hears him, leaves the man in the road and comes towards him.

Even though it looks bad, we also see Father Gabriel's progress. He is now stripped not only of his collar, but also of his pastoral jacket. Dressed only in pants and a white shirt, more of his professional armor is removed.

Random Thought

You gotta feel sorry for walkers, who are all completely ADD. Any of them can be dining on a perfectly good meal, but given a sound, a bright light or movement, and they're off to the races! "Boy, I have food right here dangling from my mouth, but I simply must respond to this new external stimulus!" Someone needs to tell them that a liver in the hand is worth two in the bush.

As the walker gets close, Father Gabriel is horrified and his survival instinct kicks in. The walker has a noose around its neck, and Father Gabriel grabs the end of the rope, pulls hard until the noose rips through the walker's neck, and its head falls off. This is the first walker that Father Gabriel has ever killed.

He then goes to the man lying in the road whose intestines have gone out to see the sights. He knows the man will never live, and he picks up a large rock and crushes the man's head. Father Gabriel may have gone outside the Alexandria walls intending to commit suicide, but for the first time, he stopped hiding and participated in the world as it is. And it devastates him. He falls down in the road, next to the dead walker and the dead man, and sobs.

When he comes back to his church, Sasha is waiting for him, drowning in anger and despair. Still wanting to escape his self-hate and having failed with the walker, he now tries suicide by pissing off a fully-armed Rickite. It is nothing he planned intellectually; his overwhelming negative emotions are driving him. Sasha asks for help, and his response is full of venom.

> SASHA: *I think I want to die.*
> FATHER GABRIEL: *Why wouldn't you want to die? You don't deserve to be here. What you did can never be undone. The dead don't choose, but the choices you made, how you sacrificed your own...*
> SASHA: *I know what you're doing.*
> FATHER GABRIEL: *Bob was mutilated, consumed, destroyed because of your sins!*
> SASHA: *Stop it!*
> FATHER GABRIEL: *Your brother felt he was apart from it—he was a part of it. He didn't deserve to be here, you don't...*
> SASHA: *Stop it! Stop it!!*

Sasha screams, rushes at him, gets him on the floor and aims her rifle. With no more heat left, he tells her simply, "Do it." But Maggie comes in looking for him to join the community meeting, and she gently puts her hand on Sasha's rifle and pulls it away. In deepest misery, unable to do anything to escape his self-hate, Father Gabriel tells his emotional truth to Maggie. He looks up and offers his second confession.

You should let her. They died…they all died because of me.

And Hershel's spiritual heir apparent gives him the most precious gift she could. She grasps his hand, helps him up, and answers him with neither judgement nor sympathy, "They did."

It is a simple acceptance of fact; as direct as her words to him on the road, but gentle. She recognizes that this second confession comes from his heart. It is, finally, his humanity. So how does she know the difference between the two confessions?

In the first confession, Father Gabriel is in full priestly garb and confesses from that position, not as a person. The first confession is chock full of excuses and defenses. The repeated phrase "I always lock the doors at night" is like saying, "It's not my fault—I was just doing my job." Locking doors is a normal evening routine and a perfectly reasonable act, but unlocking them in the morning is hardly an insurmountable challenge. It's like he's blaming the doors themselves for staying locked.

He also says, "And it was so early, it was so early." Really? He couldn't save his flock because he's not a morning person? He couldn't be bothered to get out of bed? Poor baby, he can't save his parishioners because he hasn't had his coffee yet? This is just reprehensible.

Finally, there is "…and there were so many." So now it is the fault of his flock for showing up in large numbers. If it had been only two or three, would he have gone to the door? Probably not, because it was still far too early to be asked to get up and unlock the doors.

While the first confession contains an apparent statement of responsibility, "You see, it was my choice," it also has all these dodges. It is a "yes, but" confession. Yes, but the doors were locked. Yes, but it was early. Yes, but there were too many people.

In the second confession, he has no jacket and collar; he has separated himself from his profession. He is just Gabriel, and his true confession is the simple fact laid bare: "They all died because of me."

There is nowhere to run from that. There is no blaming of routine, or the time of day, or the number of congregants, or the state of the doors. It is a human statement, the words of a man honestly unburdening his soul. And it marks Father Gabriel's full acceptance of this act, his "worst thing" in the apocalypse, the thing that makes him just like everyone else who has survived; not above them or different.

Maggie knows there is no evil in his heart. He has been a coward, yes, but not a bully or a predator. She is the right person to intervene at that moment because she has been part of Father Gabriel's journey since he joined the group. But I don't think that Sasha would have shot him, anyway. She is not a murderer; she would have ultimately pulled the gun away. And if any other Rickites had arrived instead of Maggie, they would have had the same response. Abraham would have used more colorful language, something like, "Mother dick! The world's a giant shitpot and we've all shit sideways just to stay vertical. Welcome to the damn club." But it would have been the same message—we've all been there. At the end of the episode, Maggie, Sasha and Father Gabriel are all holding hands, praying. It is a beautiful resolution.

Redemption is possible. Growth is possible. Reclaiming the wholeness of our soul is possible. We have all done things. We've lost our tempers, we've gone back to bad habits, we've hurt other people, we've let other people down, and we've let ourselves down. We've not solved our issues by the time we think we should have, and we've kept life itself at arm's length.

Because of this, we often have near-constant low levels of self-criticism. These messages play a debilitating hum just beneath the surface of our consciousness, and we live with this undercurrent of negative thoughts for years. Sometimes, sadly, they are taught to us by the adults around us when we were young. But regardless of how they came about, they are not the end of the story. Guilt and self-criticism are not the core of who we are, any more than jealousy or anger. We have to work through them. Like anger and pain, it's great if we can eradicate them, but even if they never leave us completely, we can still lessen their impact and put them behind us; in their proper place, not as something that blocks our light.

There is one final lesson that Father Gabriel teaches us. Letting go of guilt and self-hate means we have accepted who we are, including our history and all of our bumps and blemishes. But accepting who we are doesn't mean going back to the hurtful behavior. Accepting our history, and then falling back into the same bad behavior, means the work isn't finished. The part that has been left out is identifying and working through the negative emotions and misguided perceptions that caused the bad behavior in the first place.

It was paralyzing fear for his own personal safety that made Father Gabriel abandon his congregation. No matter how much he accepts responsibility for that act, he must face this fear in order to become whole again. If he doesn't, that fear could lead him to make the same mistakes again.

Father Gabriel first shows us that he has changed in 608, "Start to Finish." As the Rickites are about to weave their way through the herd in Alexandria (wearing bedsheets covered in walker guts), Father Gabriel tells Rick, "I'm not gonna give up out there. I will not turn back, no matter what happens." He is ready to face the fear for his own physical safety, because he knows that the whole group depends on everyone working together. In 609, "No Way Out," he extends his new bravery further when the journey is too much for baby Judith, and he offers to take her back to the safety of the church, walking through the herd by himself.

Father Gabriel's fear is vanquished completely in 609 when the Alexandria community fights the herd together. After Carl's eye is shot out and he is brought to the infirmary, Rick goes back out with only an axe, ready to take on the herd alone in a hail of fury. Michonne joins him once she knows Carl is safe, and other Rickites who have sought refuge in houses see the battle through the windows and go out to

Great Moments

Danai Gurira does a wonderful job starting Michonne as a walled-off warrior, then gradually and subtly opening her up. Her strength is no less, but her new friendships and love have helped her recover her willingness to connect. In 609, after Ron shoots Carl and she kills Ron, she runs ahead of Rick with her katana flying and slashing, clearing a path through the walkers so Rick can run safely behind her with Carl in his arms as they make their way to the infirmary.

The look on Michonne's face is marvelous. Is the fear for Carl there? Absolutely. Is the fierceness there? Absolutely. And so is love. It is clear there is only one thing on her mind: Save Carl. It is far more than a picture of battle. It is a picture of family.

join the fight. In a beautiful segment showing the final bonding of the Alexandrians with the Rickites, the sheltered members of Alexandria come out of their houses to finally defend themselves.

In the church, Father Gabriel looks out and sees the group fighting together, makes up his mind, and picks up a machete. Tobin asks what he is doing, and he tells the congregants calmly and with a small smile:

> *We have been praying together, praying that God will save our town. Well, our prayers have been answered. God will save Alexandria, because God has given us the courage to save it ourselves.*

Father Gabriel has not only defeated his self-hate and accepted his past, he has defeated the fear that was the origin of his problems in the first place. He has realigned himself with God on Hershel's level. He has discovered faith from the inside.

Faith is not about text and rules; it is about becoming the best of ourselves, letting go of fear and anger, and by that lifting our spirits up to the Divine (again, by whatever name we call it). Father Gabriel can now return to the traditional manifestations of faith—the Bible, a church, a collar—with new appreciation. He will still be a priest and will pass on spiritual teachings, but with a different understanding. He knows now that verses, collars, robes and rituals provide wonderful support and reminders, but they are not the true destination. His own faith, his own inner connection with the Divine, is the point. As it is for all of us.

Rick, Maggie and Daryl

In 201, Rick talks to the statue of Christ in the church.

I guess you already know I'm not much of a believer. I guess I just chose to put my faith elsewhere—my family mostly. My friends. My job.

With Rick, we see that faith can be present without an acknowledgement of belief in God. And Rick has more faith than he realizes. Rick's faith is that things will work out, and that you have to act as if they will. He may eventually come to believe in some form of Divinity, but for now his faith is in Life. His faith is definite, action-oriented and determined, and he negates any notion of giving up. As with the bearers of light, he goes through great challenges to this view. But his positive outlook pulls good people to him, and they in turn remind him to hold on to his best self, and support him in this action-faith quest. At the end of Season 6, his faith faces its biggest challenge in Negan. We have yet to see how he will respond, and we hope he will not cross over a line and become too far gone.

Another character who has the potential to become a major faith figure is Maggie. Maggie learned spirituality from her father, so she learned the text as well as faith beyond the text. In 203, "Save the Last One," Glenn asks if she believes in God and she tells him, "I always took it on faith." But in the apocalypse she goes through doubt. She tells Glenn, "Everything that's happened, there must have been a lot of praying going on and it seems quite a few went unanswered." And she tells Father Gabriel on the road, "My daddy was religious. I used to be." Despite this, she is the primary witness to Father Gabriel's spiritual journey, and ends up praying with him and Sasha in the Season 5 finale. So her faith, in whatever form she now holds it, is still there.

In Season 6 she plays a more prominent leadership role. She works with Deanna to plan crops for Alexandria, and in 605, "Now," we learn that she is pregnant. She takes on the negotiations with the Hilltop community and becomes a stronger military figure. She is perfectly situated to surpass her father's role and become a leader/warrior-priestess/Earth Mother figure. I would cheer to see her move in this direction.

As a faith figure, Daryl is the alternative voice. What, you ask? Daryl is a spiritual figure? Yes, absolutely. There is a definite non-mainstream, mythological and spiritual theme that belongs to the one and only, Daryl Dixon.

This spiritual theme for Daryl begins and ends with the search for Sophia. His own journey, and his full acceptance as a member of the Rickite tribe, occurs as he looks for this lost little girl. In Season 1, even though he is with the group, he is basically an outsider. He is the uneducated redneck, Merle's brother, the one who won't see reason. When we first meet him in 103, "Tell It to the Frogs," the other members of the camp look at him with slight scorn or mild amusement as he repeatedly kicks the downed walker who chewed up the deer he shot, calling it a "filthy, disease-bearing, motherless, poxied bastard." And the scorn is mutual. When Dale tries to calm him down, Daryl tells him, "What do you know about it, old man? Why don't you take that stupid hat and go back to *On Golden Pond*?" Daryl's loyalty is solely to Merle at this point, and he responds with physical attacks when angered. But it is not true that he won't be reasonable. Rick sees this, appeals to it, and thus begins the slow but sure journey to the strong friendship between these two men.

The first indications of Daryl's outsider spirituality are two quotes in 202, "Bloodletting," in which several Rickites are searching for Sophia in the woods. Andrea tells Carol that they are all praying with her, and Daryl responds:

It's a waste of time, all this hoping and praying. We're going to locate that little girl, and she's gonna be just fine. Am I the only one Zen around here?

It's not that Daryl is a Buddhist. But Zen Buddhism does not require any sacred texts, prayers or devotions to an Ultimate Being. Zen says that we all have the Buddha nature inside and are capable of Enlightenment, and that spiritual knowledge can come from all aspects of life. A Zen proverb states, "Before enlightenment, chop wood, carry water. After enlightenment, chop wood, carry water."[3] So, says Daryl, let's go find Sophia.

Daryl gives a second Eastern reference in 203, when he and Andrea are looking for Sophia alone at night. Andrea is doubtful they will have any success, and Daryl counters her, "It ain't the mountains of Tibet. It's Georgia."

Tibet is a Buddhist country, the home of the Dalai Lama before the Chinese invaded and he had to flee his own country. (The Dalai Lama, when he is not traveling the world, makes his home in Dharamsala, India.)[4] Given the extraordinary *TWD* writing and Daryl's earlier reference to Zen Buddhism, I don't think it's an accident that Daryl mentions this country.

Daryl also delves into Native American traditions as he comforts Sophia's mother. He gives Carol a Cherokee Rose, and tells her the significance of this flower. As the legend goes, when the Cherokee were forced along the Trail of Tears, many children were dying and their mothers grieved and cried. The elders prayed for a sign that would lift the spirits of the mothers, and these white roses with gold in the middle began to bloom where the tears of the mothers fell. Seeing this miracle, the women felt beautiful and strong, and knew they would have the

---

3 http://zenhabits.net/doing/
4 http://www.dalailama.com/biography/a-brief-biography

strength to raise the children who lived as part of a new Cherokee Nation.[5] Daryl uses this mystical legend to give Carol hope, and it marks the beginning of his strong relationship with her.

Daryl also sees a chupacabra prior to the apocalypse. Seeing visions of a chupacabra is not exactly a spiritual experience, any more than seeing a yeti or sasquatch. But it does indicate a psyche that is open to alternative mythical experiences. It shows a willingness to be receptive to nontraditional beliefs.

A more purely spiritual experience is the vision of his brother in 205. I am not an expert on Native American traditions, but it seems that Daryl's search for Sophia has elements of a vision quest.[6] He looks for Sophia more than any other character. On his last journey, he pushes himself physically, falls off his horse and tumbles down a ravine. He is injured, bruised and battered from the fall and pierced through the side by one of his own arrows. He is weak, with his consciousness only partly in this world. He sees his brother, Merle, who we know is not physically there. The Merle vision tells him, "Why don't you pull that arrow out, dummy? You could bind your wound better."

Merle pushes and prods Daryl in classic Merle fashion, giving him the strength to climb up the embankment. We typically think that visions encountered during a vision quest should be noble; Cree Indian William Sacred received visitations from spirits in the form of sparks of light, and from his deceased father.[7] Merle is hardly noble, but the vision is of someone who has been the closest to Daryl so far. Vision-Merle saves Daryl's life, and gives Daryl direction and purpose not in the form of guidance, but in a way that is similar to what Tyreese experienced at his death. Daryl is challenged by vision-Merle to defend his new way of being and to stand up for his relationship with Rick.

Daryl does defend his new self, and he comes back from his quest changed. He brings back to the community the closest thing they

5 http://www.firstpeople.us/FP-Html-Legends/LegendOfTheCherokeeRose-Cherokee.html

6 https://www.warpaths2peacepipes.com/native-american-culture/vision-quest.htm

7 http://native-americans-online.com/native-american-vision.html

ever get to Sophia as she used to be—her doll. The innocent toy of an innocent child. (Appropriately, the only person to criticize this accomplishment is Shane.) Daryl has left his old self behind in order to retrieve it. He emerges from the woods, limping back to the farm, bloody and haggard, so unrecognizable that he is mistaken by Andrea for a walker and shot. (No surprises here—Andrea is hardly a character of clear vision.)

As he lays in a guest bedroom bruised and bandaged, Sophia's mother comes in and offers the true reward for this completion of his inner journey:

> CAROL: *You need to know something. You did more for my little girl today than her own daddy ever did in his whole life.*
> DARYL: *I didn't do anything Rick or Shane wouldn't have done.*
> CAROL: *I know. You're every bit as good as them. Every bit.*

With this, Carol has officially brought him into the group. She has acknowledged his equality with the leaders and warriors. His acceptance is sealed.

When Sophia does appear, she is already a walker, and Daryl grieves along with the rest of the Rickites. But the point was the search. It gave him purpose and it bonded him with Carol. As Sophia emerges from the barn, Daryl is now officially Carol's protector, holding her as she sinks to the ground, sobbing.

Daryl Dixon took on a quest, going outside the box in his search for Sophia and himself. He accepts experiences that would make others scoff. If he ever goes on another inner journey, it may include ley lines, a leather pouch containing herbs, crystals and a wolf's tooth for protection, and a spirit animal. It is a good sign for the Rickites. Any healthy society will have people who trust in nontraditional spirituality and outside-the-box experiences, and they stand as a testament to its openness and freedom.

3

When Does the Killing Go Too Far?

We don't kill the living.
—Rick, 105, "Wildfire"

*Not for one second do I think there is malice in your heart. You're not
a killer and I know that. I know that. So do whatever you gotta do to
keep this group safe, and do it with a clear conscience.*
—Lori to Rick, 302, "Sick"

It's not over till they're all dead.
—Rick, 501, "No Sanctuary"

Lori is right. There is no malice in Rick's heart, even now. Toughness
yes, malice, no. There is debate in the *TWD* fan world over whether
any members of our intrepid group have gone too far in their killing.
Most of the questions revolve around Rick, and it is true that he has
become the most accepting of the need to kill and aggressive in attacking
those who are a threat. He has also come the closest to crossing ethical
lines in killing. On the other hand, Carol has become so horrified at
her own body count that she exiles herself from Alexandria so she won't
have to kill to save the people she loves. And Morgan decided not to
kill anyone at all, even if they are a threat.

So who is right? When does the killing go too far? I believe it depends
on two issues: whether you have crossed the line into becoming a
predator, or whether you have killed callously for selfish reasons.

In the *TWD* world, killing can be awful, life-changing, tear-shedding, PTSD-causing, wall-building horrendous. But as long as you haven't gone to predator land or killed for selfish reasons, it's a hard but necessary decision, often made quickly in the middle of a battle or a rescue.

In this chapter, we'll examine several categories of *TWD* killing. First we will review killing as reactive self-defense, killing as proactive self-defense, and killing as a predator. We'll look at neutrality, in which you don't want to kill people, but you have their blood on your hands anyway. Two examples of this are Andrea and Morgan, for different reasons. We'll look at killing through inaction, as with Orange Backpack Guy, and at the difference between being brutal and being predatory. We'll examine the kill history for Rick and Carol. And finally, we'll look at two special situations: Shane's killing of Otis and Carol's killing of Karen and David.

Killing as Reactive Self-Defense

Look, we can settle this; we're reasonable men. First we're gonna beat Daryl to death. Then we'll have the girl. Then the boy. Then I'm gonna shoot you and then we'll be square.
–Joe, 416, "A"

Reactive self-defense is when you are face to face with an immediate threat or have been recently under attack. (And self-defense also includes defense of your community.) Examples of this are when the Governor rolls up to the prison and starts firing, or in Terminus when Rick, Bob, Daryl and Glenn are lined up by the trough as the Terminians prepare to cut their throats, bleed them out, and filet them for the barbeque. It also includes the attack of Joe and the Claimers on Rick, Michonne, Daryl and Carl; the invasion of the Wolves into Alexandria; the surviving Terminians hunting the Rickites; and Maggie and Carol's capture by Paula and the Saviors.

Killing as Proactive Self-Defense

We try and talk to the Saviors, we give up our advantage, our safety. No. We have to come for them before they come for us.
–Rick, 612, "Not Tomorrow Yet"

Killing as proactive self-defense involves preventing an attack that would undoubtedly happen. Proactive self-defense should always be considered very carefully and should never be used without absolute certainty that the people you plan to attack present a lethal and continuing threat. If they are not predators, if they are also just trying to stay alive and engaging in proactive self-defense, then rational discussion

Great Monologues

Michael Rooker as Merle gives a wonderful, desperate, angry rooftop monologue in 103. Alone and handcuffed to a pipe, Merle goes from dehydrated, story-telling delirium to sharp fear when he sees walkers clawing their way through the chained stairwell door.

Please, oh, Jesus, please, I know, I know I'm being punished, I know. Oh, I deserve it, I deserve it, I deserve it! Tell me now, show me the way. Tell me, tell me what to do. Tell me, tell me! Oh, God!

When he realizes he can reach an abandoned hacksaw with his belt, instead of offering gratitude for an answered prayer, he regresses back to his true nature.

That's okay. Never you mind, sonny Christ boy. I ain't begged you before, I ain't going to start begging now. I ain't gonna beg you now! Don't you worry 'bout me begging you ever!

Michael brings the delirium, terror and rage all seamlessly together. Shoulda gotta Emmy.

and negotiated solutions may be possible and should be explored. But if you know for a fact that you are facing a predator leader and his or her group, then proactive self-defense is not only acceptable, it is necessary.

In Season 6, the Rickite attack on the Savior compound is a prime example of proactive self-defense. Carol has used proactive self-defense, both at the prison and the grove. But there have also been times in *TWD* when proactive self-defense would have been a good idea, but wasn't pursued.

There are two missed opportunities to kill the Governor. The first is in 310, "Home," after the rescue mission that saves Maggie and Glenn from their captivity at Woodbury. Back home at the safety of the prison, Glenn and Michonne want to go back to Woodbury to assassinate the Governor, but Hershel says no.

The second missed opportunity to kill the Governor happens in 311, after the first attack on the prison. Andrea comes to the prison from Woodbury to promote negotiations (give me a break) for the two groups. But the Rickites do not trust their former friend, who is literally sleeping with the enemy. When they are alone, Carol calmly tells Andrea to go back to Woodbury, go to bed with the Governor, and kill him in his sleep.

Andrea considers it. She does have sex with the Governor, and after he is asleep she gets out of bed, gets a knife and goes toward him. But she can't do it. Thus spared a second time, the Governor goes on to destroy the prison.

The Rickites also reject proactive self-defense after they escape Terminus. Once they are safe outside the Terminus fence, Rick wants to continue the fight. The rest object, but not because of ethics. It's only because they don't want to risk their lives again. As Abraham says, "I'm not dickin' around with this crap. We just made it out."

It was probably a wise decision not to go back into a flaming herd of walkers and angry Terminians. But if the Rickites had decided to finish off Gareth and his crew, Bob wouldn't have had to witness his own leg being consumed, and other unknown victims would have been spared.

As Gareth tells Bob in 502, "We would have done this to anybody. We will." Also, the Rickite decision not to go back into Terminus only postponed the inevitable. The Terminians followed them, hunted them, and the Rickites had to finish the fight with the cannibals at St. Sarah's church, anyway.

The most tragic example of proactive self-defense is Carol's killing of Lizzie. After Lizzie stabs her sister, Carol recognizes that there is no way to handle Lizzie's insanity. Lizzie sees nothing wrong with killing people to make them into walkers; she is an ongoing threat. Carol and Tyreese discuss their options. They talk about separating, with one of them taking Judith and the other staying with Lizzie. But they know that neither of them would make it alone with a baby, and Lizzie would still be a danger to herself and whoever she was with.

So Carol shoots the young teenage girl. It is proactive self-defense, and sadly, in the *TWD* world, there simply wasn't another choice.

Rick's killing of Shane is somewhere between reactive and proactive self-defense. Shane takes Rick out into the field to kill him, so Rick was acting in immediate self-defense. But Rick is honest, and he tells Lori later that he could have solved the situation another way and didn't because "I just wanted it over." But Rick is being too hard on himself because Shane was delusional by that time; he wanted Rick dead and wanted Lori and Carl for himself. He would have tried to kill Rick again sometime, anyway.

The nighttime attack on the Savior compound is proactive self-defense. Some fans have said this attack made the Rickites no different than the Saviors. I disagree, because at the time of this attack, Rick and company already know that the Saviors prey on other groups. They learn from Jesus at the Hilltop community that the Saviors showed up at their gates, demanded half of their supplies, and beat a sixteen-year-old boy to death in front of them. They also know that it was the Saviors who tried to attack Daryl, Abraham and Sasha on the road. After experiencing the Governor, the Claimers and the Terminians, Rick doesn't want to wait around for the attack he knows will come.

In attacking the Savior compound, the main problem wasn't crossing over any ethical lines—it was lack of good intelligence. They thought that the satellite compound was home for all of the Saviors, and they were badly mistaken.

Killing as a Predator

If it makes you feel any better, you taste much better than we thought you would.
—Gareth, 502, "Strangers"

Take off your shirt or I'll bring Glenn's hand in here.
—The Governor, 307, "When the Dead Come Knocking"

Anybody moves, anybody says anything, cut the boy's other eye out and feed it to his father. And then we'll start.
—Negan, 616, "Last Day on Earth"

If you are a predator, you kill people who have done you no harm and have presented no threat. It is not self-defense, it is murder. No one in Rick's group has entered this territory. Not one. Ever. Period.

With no government, police, or legal systems, there are ample predators to go around. One of the most important survival skills in *TWD* is knowing how to recognize one. (It's a pretty important survival skill in our world, too.) So how do we do this? Here are some predator qualities. They don't all need to be present for someone to qualify as a predator, but a true predator will have most.

Predators Never Stop Attacking

Repeated attacks are a mandatory factor to qualify as a predator. This is true of all serial killers; *serial* by definition means multiple. If someone injures or murders only once, it may be for other reasons—vengeance, jealousy, unchecked rage, etc. This makes the person a criminal, but not a predator. Only with repeated behavior does the predator label apply. All the predators in *TWD* attack repeatedly until they are forcibly stopped.

Predators Seek Opportunities to Kill People

Predators don't need provocation—they are happy to attack or kill innocent victims. Negan's gangs search out new communities to subdue, killing one of the community members just to make a point. The Wolves slaughter entire neighborhoods, and the Wolf Leader tells Morgan that he meets new people every two weeks or so because, "Oh, I work at it." They look for people to kill. And the Terminians, while they don't pursue their prey, act as spiders who lure flies into their web. Predators may claim self-defense, but it is a ruse to cover their preference for killing as a method to achieve control. Or heck, just to make it a better day for them.

There is one person in *TWD* who has killed innocent people on multiple occasions and is not a predator: Morgan. Morgan is an ordinary person who went a bit crazy; the writing all over the walls in the room where Rick, Michonne and Carl find him is testament to that. But Morgan has also spray-painted warning signs all over the buildings and grounds where he is staying: "Away with you," "Turn around and live," "Not shitting you." This is not only an attempt to keep himself safe from dangerous invaders into his space; it is also an effort, made by a barely-there vestige of his former self, to keep people away so he won't have to kill them. None of the predators in *TWD* would consider such a thing.

Morgan didn't look for opportunities to kill; he only killed people who crossed his path. He never got callous about killing or did so for selfish reasons. In the midst of his despair, he wanted to be killed himself. These are not the characteristics of a predator.

Predators Can Be Charming

Predators can be perfectly nice. When we first meet Joe in 413, we don't know whether to like him or not. He is charming in his own rough way. He is educated, knows who Charles Darwin is and how to use the word *oblongata* correctly in a sentence. Joe has a code—don't steal, don't lie. But we soon discover that lying is a capital offense, that "teach him all the way" means beat the person to death, and that Joe and his group roam the countryside raping and murdering at will. Joe's affable style covers true menace, and his joke to Daryl, "Why hurt yourself when you can hurt other people," is no joke at all.

The Governor fools members of his own community with his smooth charm. They have no idea that he keeps heads in aquarium tanks and kills people to get their supplies. He gives the citizens a good speech, provides food and entertainment and they think he is a good leader. (Although there are reasons to suspect him, and Michonne picks up on all of them.)

The Terminus entry is decorated with growing plants, laundry tubs, and other folksy items depicting a happy hearth and home. Gareth's mother, Mary, smiles and greets newcomers at the front entrance. She offers warm sympathy and prepares a plate of meat for them, fresh off the barbeque. Gareth is perfectly polite in 416 when four of the Rickites saunter into the back entrance of one of the Terminus buildings.

> GARETH: *Welcome to Terminus. I'm Gareth. Looks like you've been on the road a for good bit.*
> RICK: *We have. Rick. That's Carl, Daryl, Michonne.*
> GARETH: *You're nervous, I get it. We were all the same way. We came here for sanctuary. That what you here for?*
> RICK: *Yes.*
> GARETH: *Good. You've found it.*

Not so much. It's all a well-acted trap. At the trough, Gareth tells his men to get the victims onto the drying racks quickly and that he's going to "go back to public face." The charm is completely contrived, and unlike in Woodbury, all of his people know it.

In our world, serial killers and other predators often use charm to lure victims. Ted Bundy wore a fake cast on his arm to make young women think he was safe; that and a handsome smile led victims to their deaths. The BTK killer in Kansas was a pillar in his community and active in his church. Predators don't necessarily appear dangerous, and recognizing them can require trusting our own intuition.

The modern world puts far, far too much focus on being "liked" and "followed." It is dangerous. We are trained to trust the most superficial of messages, and not to question or listen to the inner voice that warns of danger. Here is a piece of advice, especially but not exclusively for young women: don't be swayed by superficial charm. Take a lesson from Michonne and listen to your gut, stay safe, and please, please, please don't worry about being liked or what people think of you when your alarm bells are clanging. Someone you meet may be charming, interesting and likeable, but that doesn't mean they are kind, good and ethical. Better to be seen as rude than end up attacked or dead.

Predators Terrorize Their Victims

This is not a mandatory quality, but the Governor certainly has it. While he is setting up a torture room, he grabs two chains hanging from posts, pulls on them, and has a reaction that is almost sexual. He enjoys the idea of torture on a visceral, physical level. He whistles into a tape recorder while equipping another room, and again as he walks through an abandoned building searching for Andrea. He wants to elicit terror in his victims, in this case with sound. Matched with a threat, a simple whistle can cause intense fear.

Whistling enters the *TWD* world again with Negan's group, initially just a few at a time as the Rickites run into his gangs while trying to get to the Hilltop. After the Rickites recognize the whistling as a sign that the Saviors are near, they are terrified by the large number of whistles surrounding them in the woods. It is eerie and creepy, and conveys no way out.

Random Thought

Who's on Lucille cleaning detail? After bashing someone's head in, there's going to be more than blood on there. There's going to be hair and skin and dangling nerves and little bits of brain all caught up in the barbs, and a quick rinse with the hose just isn't gonna do it. Someone's going to have to get in there with tweezers and a toothbrush. Yuck.

Negan takes pleasure in knowing that he can terrorize people. When he meets the Rickites in 616, he flashes a big smile and greets them with:

Pissin' our pants yet? Boy, do I have a feelin' we're gettin' close. Yeah. It's gonna be pee-pee pants city here real soon.

Terror is part of subduing people, and Negan again deliberately uses it as he takes his time choosing which Rickite he will beat to death with his barbed-wire wrapped baseball bat, Lucille.

Gareth doesn't care about torture—he just wants to get the job done. He is an efficiency geek, asking about "shot counts" and inventorying which victims came from which train cars. Every task—from repeating the radio message to killing people at the trough—is just part of making the whole operation run smoothly. Nothing more, nothing less.

Certainly, being the victim of any predator is going to be terrifying. But some of them revel in it more than others.

Predators Assume Ownership

The best example of this is Negan. He assumes ownership of anything around him and takes from people who are trying to rebuild their own little corner of the world. As he says plainly in 616:

The new world order is this—and it's really very simple, so even if you're stupid, which you very may well be, you can understand it. You ready? Here goes, pay attention. Give me your shit, or I will kill you.

Other prominent takers include Joe and the Claimers. Joe has developed a system for who gets what: all a member of the gang has to do is say "claimed" to own a desired item, whether a jacket, a can of soup, or an old blanket. When we first encounter Joe and the Claimers in 411, "Claimed," we hear them enter a house where Rick, Michonne and Carl are staying. Rick is alone in the house and quickly hides under a bed upstairs. The voices are muffled, but we hear the word *claimed* repeatedly. The Claimers don't know whether someone is staying in the house, whether any occupants are gone or whether they will return, but it doesn't matter. The stuff in the house is theirs, regardless.

We find out that claiming includes people when we hear these male voices discussing Michonne's shirt. One of the Claimers finds a woman's shirt freshly washed, and they figure whoever owns it will be back. Another says immediately, "I call first when she gets here." He has called the right to rape her first. Not only; just first. Inside of five minutes, we know everything we need to know about this group. They are brutal and they see the world as theirs to take by force.

Gareth and his group obviously claim ownership of anyone who comes to Terminus. Gareth no longer sees people as fellow human beings; they are his to use and consume, and their belongings are kept in a warehouse for distribution among the Terminus community.

Assumed ownership is not exclusive to predators—other *TWD* characters have shown this trait. Mitch, a member of the Governor's second group, complains when his decent older brother Pete won't let their hunting group attack another camp and steal their supplies. On their way back, they find everyone in this camp dead or dying and the supplies gone. When Pete chides Mitch for thinking about the supplies before the people, Mitch responds angrily, "Damn right they're dead! That was gonna happen either way! Now some other group's got our stuff!" *Our* stuff. To him, it always was.

Compare this to Daryl's attitude about the "white trash brunch" at the funeral home. When he realizes that "This is someone's stash," he says that they will take just some and leave the rest. Food and supplies are necessary to survive, but Daryl honors the survival needs of others, as well.

Predators don't build; they take because they feel it is their due. If they want it, it's theirs.

Predator Leaders Require Total Control

Predator leaders will not put up with competition, either from the leader of another group, or from inside their own. They run the show, period, and require total control.

In 303, "Walk With Me," the Governor finds a National Guard helicopter crashed in a field. Only one pilot is still alive, and he is brought back to Woodbury. The Governor tricks him into revealing where the other National Guard soldiers are located, then kills him and adds his head to the aquarium tank collection. The Governor drives up to the other soldiers waving a white napkin. When the soldiers let down their guard and their weapons, the Governor's men come out of the bushes and open fire.

The Governor does this to take their weapons and supplies, but it is not just an assumption of ownership; it is also refusal to allow any competition. How so? Killing the soldiers makes no sense. Why not make them allies? Wouldn't trained soldiers be a tremendous asset in protecting your community? This is what the Rickites would do, after vetting them with the three questions.

But the Governor's personal prime directive is not to strengthen his community; it is to bring in people he can control. This could be difficult with members of the military, who might still hold loyalty to any vestige of the United States and values that include integrity, honesty and freedom. It would be like trying to control Abraham, who actually wants to save the world, not take advantage of its weakness.

Predators have an instinct for reading people and knowing who is controllable and who isn't. The Governor kills Pete, who is a leader in his second group, but brings Mitch into the fold. He takes Andrea under his wing, but knows Michonne is a threat. His Woodbury inner circle includes Merle, Shump and Martinez, who he sensed were tough enough to do his killing, but not strong enough to be competitive leaders. It's a skill, of sorts. And the Governor uses it fully.

Negan makes people kneel in front of him and enforces brutal punishments for breaking his rules. Everyone defers to him completely. In addition, the statements from other Saviors like Molls in 613 that "we are all Negan," sounds creepy and cult-like. It makes people feel strong to be associated with a strongman, but when someone gives themselves over like that, they no longer truly exist as an individual. The Saviors have lost the option of making up their own mind, and Negan has total control.

Predator Leaders Will Turn Against Their Own People

Predators have no loyalty except to their own power. The Governor shoots his own people after they retreat from the second attack on the prison. He kills his longtime friend and advisor, Milton. He kills Andrea, who he supposedly cared about romantically. He (unsuccessfully) pits Merle against Daryl in a gladiator fight to the death in 309, "The Suicide King," and finally kills Merle in 315, "This Sorrowful Life." Doing good work for a predator leader doesn't guarantee your safety.

We haven't seen Negan turn against his own people, yet, Governor-style. Brutal punishment for breaking the rules is not exactly the same. However, I'm sure if Negan got upset with his people, Lucille would happily come out to play.

Random Thought

Is there a reason that Negan's baseball bat bears the same name as B.B. King's guitar? Just wondering. Only Robert Kirkman knows for sure.

Predators Lie and Deceive

This isn't a mandatory quality. Joe doesn't lie or deceive. Negan and the Saviors don't lie. Right off the bat (get it?), they'll openly tell you their plans.

The Governor is quite active in his lies. When he and his men bring the National Guard jeeps back to Woodbury, he tells his citizens that the soldiers were overrun by walkers. When several of the Governor's men die in the attempt to find and kill Michonne in 306, Merle asks how to explain their deaths. The Governor tell him, "We'll dress it up; give 'em a hero's funeral. You tell a story—a supply run gone sideways." For the Governor, lying to his people is standard operating procedure.

The Terminians lie as they lure people to them with the "Sanctuary for All" signs and the repeated Terminus radio broadcast that states, "Those who arrive, survive." Once newcomers do arrive and the lie is exposed, they either join the lies or go to the trough.

Predators Don't Let Anyone Leave

This also isn't a mandatory quality, although it is true for most of our *TWD* predators. The only exception is Joe, who doesn't force people to stay with the group. He tries to convince Daryl to stay, but there are no threats to Daryl when he wants to leave.

At Terminus, those who arrive and agree to be cannibals do survive and don't appear to be forced to stay. But it would be safe to assume that having someone abandon ship isn't something Gareth would want. The escapee could warn others to stay away and eliminate the food supply. Rick did this when he changed a "Sanctuary for All" sign to "No Sanctuary for All."

The one who most actively blocks freedom of movement is the Governor, and everyone in Woodbury knows this rule. The Governor claims a benevolent desire to protect his people from the dangers outside, but it is just another lie to his people. Michonne understands this immediately, and when the Governor does let her go, it is a ruse to fool Andrea.

Finally, at Grady Memorial Hospital, Dawn and the former cops who work for her rescue people, bring them to the hospital to heal any injuries, and use the concept of "owing" to keep them as indentured servants.

In our world, no North Koreans can leave their own country without government permission, and are limited in their movements even within North Korea.[8] The same was true in the old Soviet Union, in which citizens needed (rare) government permission to leave the country, and refusing to return was deemed treason.[9] While travel bans were lifted with Russia's 1993 constitution, in recent years the restrictions have crept back in again. The Russian leadership has banned foreign travel for many government workers, as well as for another large chunk of the population—people who are in debt. The government can deny international travel to any of its citizens who owe taxes or have outstanding bank loans, alimony, or fees. Russia maintains a "debtor's database," and authorities detain people in airports or train stations.[10] Cuba has eased its decades long travel restrictions as of January 2013, which is a wonderful step forward for Cubans. But the government can still deny travel to those it considers crucial to national security, a category which includes doctors, scientist and engineers. Also, the average wage in Cuba is $18 a month, and the cost of a passport equals five months of salary.[11]

Freedom to leave a country and come back at will is a strong barometer of the overall quality of life for its citizens. If there is slim to no freedom in this area, there is probably precious little freedom in other areas, either. And any country in which the government blocks its own citizens' ability to leave probably has a dictator in power.

---

8 http://www.libertyinnorthkorea.org/learn-nk-challenges/

9 https://en.wikipedia.org/wiki/Human_rights_in_the_Soviet_Union

10 http://foreignpolicy.com/2016/04/29/in-russia-the-doors-are-closing-tourism-putin-human-rights/

11 http://www.usatoday.com/story/news/world/2012/11/11/cuba-exit-visas/1694569/

Predators Can't "Come Back"

Once you have preyed on and killed innocent people, it is almost impossible to "come back" to who you were before, and the predators themselves know it. They say it.

Gareth admits that he can't go back when Bob tells him that the Rickites know someone who can cure the virus. The Governor thinks Rick's plea that they can learn to live together is a lie, showing that he is too far gone to come back and see reason. And Joe never thought he went anywhere in the first place. He doesn't see the apocalypse as the world falling apart, but instead tells Daryl in 415 that "things are finally starting to fall together."

As of the end of Season 6, the question of "coming back" hasn't come up with Negan. But Negan is a true predator who is drenched in blood and has created a community run by obedience, theft, death and punishment. His soul is hardened, and it doesn't look like he has any desire to change a thing. If someone naively told him he could come back, he would probably laugh and ask why he should.

So What Do You Do About It?

When you know how to recognize a predator, what do you do when faced with one? Predators can't be ignored. Closing your eyes and hoping they will go away won't work. You have to stop them, get away from them, render them harmless, take away their power, or isolate them. You have to basically do whatever it takes to end the terror they create.

You have to be strong in yourself, know who you are and be comfortable with it. If you are filled with self-doubt and a need for approval, it will cloud your vision. If you think that compassionate action is only warm and fuzzy, it will cloud your vision. If your need for self-preservation is so great that it stops you from taking risks, that will also cloud your vision. All of these responses lead to inaction, and that can be fatal.

Listen to your gut and act on it. Don't listen to your brain, because your brain can rationalize anything. Don't listen to your heart, because your heart will take you on a trip. But your gut will talk straight with you, if you will only listen. And other people will tell you who they are, if you will only listen. So listen.

Most of the Rickites listen to their instincts and respond appropriately to predators. The prime example of this is Michonne. She knows who she is, is comfortable with who she is, and listens to her gut. When she and Andrea meet the Governor, Michonne sees him clearly. Her alarm bells start going off the minute he takes away their weapons and posts guards at the door of their room. Her suspicions multiply when he continually offers reasons why she and Andrea shouldn't leave, and the deal is sealed when she finds bullet holes in the National Guard jeeps, which reveal the Governor's lie that the soldiers got overrun by a walker herd. Michonne desperately tries to convince Andrea, but when it doesn't work, Michonne leaves on her own. She is true to her gut and takes action based on what it is telling her, even though her heart aches over leaving her friend.

Your gut can also tell you when people are decent. When Michonne witnesses Maggie and Glenn being kidnapped by Merle, she takes the baby formula that they drop and goes to the prison. After hearing Maggie and Glenn talk, she senses that they are good people who may come from a good group. She finds the Rickites because she listened to her gut when it gave her a positive message (and the reward of a loving relationship with Carl and Rick is greater than she could have imagined).

If you decide to ignore a predator, trauma inevitably follows. Predators won't stop. Neutrality and half-measures won't work. Predators laugh in the face of half-measures, and will simply take advantage of people who aren't willing to deal with them head-on. This brings us to the dangers of neutrality.

Neutrality

I just didn't want anyone to die.
—Andrea, 316, "Welcome to the Tombs"

All life is precious.
—Morgan, 607, "Heads Up"

Aren't those quotes nice? Shouldn't we all aspire to that? Yes, whenever possible. But there are times in our world, as in *TWD*, when refusing to take sides isn't realistic and neutrality becomes a form of killing.

The person who does the neutrality dance when dealing with a predator is nothing more than a predator enabler, because the time taken up with neutrality allows the predator to continue on his (or her) murderous ways. If someone is against killing predators (and they are living in the apocalypse with no law enforcement, mental hospitals or prisons), then they either don't recognize predators or simply don't want to deal with what it takes to stop them. They have a head full of fluff and wouldn't listen to their gut if it jumped out of their stomach, flew up in front of their face and started screaming at them. The two people who epitomize neutrality are Andrea and Morgan, for different reasons.

Andrea

With no offense to actress Laurie Holden, Andrea annoyed me more than any other character. First she's suicidal, then she's all tough guns and "Shane for President," then she's playing Secretary General of the United Nations and trying to broker peace in our time for Rick and the Governor. Good Lord, woman, who are you? She can't answer because, unfortunately for herself and many other *TWD* characters, she doesn't know. When you don't know who you are and don't listen to your gut, you can be easily led. Your judgement can get lost in your need for someone. You can be what we would call co-dependent, and that is Andrea.

The Governor is not the first man who Andrea misjudges. She has sex with Shane in a car, feeling frisky after she figures out how to successfully aim her pistol. When they get back to the farm, she smiles shyly like a schoolgirl, as if having sex with Shane somehow meant that he liked her. We're talking Shane here. Yes, he and Andrea formed a bit of an alliance in Season 2. But as far as man and woman go, Shane's romantic delusions are aimed at Lori and Andrea was nothing more than a bump and grind in the road. But her view of people is as faulty as when she thought Daryl was a walker and shot him.

Andrea spent months with the Rickites and knows they are good people, but all of that leaves her head once she meets the Governor. She puts the Governor and her former friends on equal moral footing, even after she knows the Governor has lied to her. Even after she sees the heads in aquarium tanks. Even after she knows that Maggie and Glenn were held captive at Woodbury. Still, she won't see Phillip for who he is.

She loses her sense of loyalty to Michonne as well. She met Michonne on the road after being run off the farm, and they survived alone together for an entire winter. They fought walkers, scrounged whatever food they could and had each other's backs. But in Andrea's desire for the Governor's approval, all that is forgotten.

Michonne takes great risks to try to expose the Governor to Andrea. She goes on the mission to rescue Glenn and Maggie, finds the Governor's secret study with the aquarium heads, kills walker-Penny and fights the Governor. But when Andrea comes in and sees the scene, her immediate response is to accuse Michonne: "What have you done?" This must have hurt Michonne terribly.

Michonne sees Andrea's problems clearly, and while Andrea is back at the prison in 311, Michonne talks straight with her.

> ANDREA: *Once we entered Woodbury, you became hostile.*
> MICHONNE: *That's 'cause I could see it.*
> ANDREA: *See what?*
> MICHONNE: *That you were under his spell from the second you laid eyes on him.*
> ANDREA: *That is not true!*
> MICHONNE: *And you still are.*

It doesn't work, and Andrea goes back to the Governor. But Michonne did everything she could. In all her actions, she thought first about Andrea's safety, even if it meant losing Andrea's friendship. That is bravery and true caring.

Even when Andrea sees the Governor's faults, she never takes a stand or does anything about it. Her heart takes her on a trip and her brain rationalizes his behavior. And like many abusive people, he knows how to push her buttons; he senses her weakness and manipulates her emotions with lines like, "You're just a visitor here. Just passing through. So why should I tell you?" He pushes her away, and she responds classically, "Don't do that. Don't drive me out." She is willing to ignore danger in order to keep her illusion. And sadly, like many abused women, she ends up dead.

It is only when she sees the Governor lay out instruments in his torture room that she is willing to admit the truth, and by then it is too late. She tries to escape Woodbury, but he follows her and catches her. She ends up handcuffed to a chair and spends the last moments of her life waiting for Milton (who is also codependently loyal to the Governor) to die, turn, and attack her.

Rick, Daryl, and Michonne find her, feverish from the walker-Milton bite. She asks Rick if the others are alive. "Judith, Carl, the rest of them…" And he corrects her. "Us. The rest of us." Andrea was with a good group of people and she could not have found a better or stronger friend than Michonne. She lost sight of all that.

Great Music

As the camera winds through the foreboding hallways of the Governor's basement, pushes through a locked door and reveals Andrea gagged and handcuffed to a chair, we hear the dark, driving, "You Are the Wilderness," by Voxhall Broadcast. It is a perfect accompaniment.

It is tempting to feel sorry for Andrea as she prepares to shoot herself in the head to prevent her own turn. But if we think about all the people who died because of her blindness and inaction, the sympathy is tempered with stark reality.

Andrea's missed opportunity to kill the Governor happened in 311. So in honor of Andrea's failure to recognize a predator and her foolish flight of neutrality fancy, here is a list of people who were killed as a direct result of the Governor's actions from the moment Andrea chose not to kill him, to when Michonne finally does in 408. The people who died because Andrea just didn't want anyone to die are:

- 6 of the Governor's soldiers at the feed store (315)
- Merle Dixon (315)
- Ben (315)
- 17 Woodbury citizens during the second prison attack (316)
- Andrea (316)
- Milton (316)
- Alan (316)
- Shumpert (unknown—sometime between these episodes)
- Martinez (407, "Dead Weight")
- Pete (407)
- 16 of the Governor's second group (408)
- Mitch (408)
- Alicia (408)
- Hershel (408)

This adds up to fifty people who died because Andrea wouldn't stop the Governor. Count 'em. Fifty people died because Andrea's head was full of fluff and she didn't recognize a predator or listen to her gut.

Predators will never stop on their own, they won't honor negotiations, and you can't talk them down or reason with them. In dealing with them, neutrality proponents need not apply.

Morgan

Morgan is also in the neutral category, but he's not like Andrea—he knows a predator when he sees one, and he knows what they will do. Morgan's problem is the terrible guilt that stems from not killing his walker-wife, the death of his son, and killing innocent people. His subsequent refusal to kill, even in self-defense, is overcompensation. It keeps him peaceful; his emotional turmoil is indeed resolved with his complete nonviolence stance. But Carol is accurate when she criticizes Morgan for not killing the Wolf Leader. "That was for you, not for us." The nonviolence works for him and is a method of coping that seems noble, but it denies the reality of the apocalypse. His "all life is precious" neutrality has devastating effects.

When we first meet Morgan, he seems to be dealing well with the apocalypse. He uses gas lanterns, nails boards on the windows and reminds his son, Duane, to stay quiet. He can kill walkers who are threatening them and stops Duane from killing Rick when Rick shows the power of speech. But when the apocalypse touches Morgan personally, he loses his nerve and good judgment. He can't bring himself to shoot his walker-wife, and because he doesn't, she later attacks their son, Duane.

The scenes in 101 in which Morgan can't shoot walker-Jenny alternate with Rick's scenes in the park with Bicycle Girl, the walker whose lower half went missing and who is growling up at him. He goes over to the walker, looks down with sympathy and says, "I'm sorry this happened to you." He then shoots her in the head.

With these scenes, we see a poignant juxtaposition of the two men—one able to adapt, the other not. Would it have been harder for Rick to shoot if it had been walker-Lori instead of a stranger? Probably, but I think he still would have done it, even if it was in pain and anguish. He would have recognized that it wasn't Lori anymore. One of Rick's strengths is his ability to adapt to new situations quickly.

The double trauma of losing Jenny and his responsibility for Duane's death sends Morgan on a path of violent madness. He spends months lashing out against the world, killing both in self-defense and not, and because he isn't a predator, killing innocent people creates incredible pain in his soul. He becomes semi-insane, but aware enough to feel the keen despair of his situation.

Morgan wanders onto Eastman's property, ready to kill him, too. They fight, and Eastman knocks him out with an aikido stick and puts him in a cell he has built inside his cabin. By the time he meets "the cheesemaker," Morgan is so despondent that when he wakes up and Eastman asks his name, he says simply, "Kill me." (Which brings us Eastman's wonderful casual response, "Well, that's a stupid name. It's dangerous. You should change it.")

Eastman was a forensic psychologist before the apocalypse. He diagnoses Morgan with PTSD, tell him that he doesn't have to kill, and offers three main arguments for nonviolence. First, that people aren't designed to kill, because we don't have fangs or claws. (He promotes vegetarianism, and offers Morgan only cheese, tomatoes, and oatmeal burgers.) Second, that soldiers who come back from war with PTSD do so because humans aren't comfortable with killing. And third, we can all change. But there are flaws in each of these arguments.

Humans have four categories of teeth—incisors, canines, premolars and molars—which means we are designed to eat both vegetables and meat. Our canine teeth and incisors are made to tear into flesh. If we

Random Thought

Ya gotta feel sorry for walkers like Bicycle Girl who are missing legs, stuck to trees, or melting into the pavement. Bicycle Girl's hunger is still there as she reaches up to Rick and snarls, but she has no clue that he can totally get away from her. If she actually had an operational frontal lobe, she would be like, "Damn! Here's food, and me with no way to stand up!"

were built to be vegetarians, our mouths would house primarily molars, like cows, to grind fibrous vegetable matter.

In addition, we have opposable thumbs to hold tools for hunting and a brain to create them. We don't need to chase our prey, pounce on it and kill it with our teeth. (Interestingly, walkers are carnivores, and this is exactly what they do.) Some of us may choose not to eat meat, but to say that we aren't meant to kill because we don't have fangs or claws is a false argument.

Secondly, the PTSD argument isn't false, but it is incomplete. I am not an expert on PTSD, but I understand that many things can cause PTSD. The entire battle experience—the noise and confusion, being in a life-threatening situation, the constant tension and fear, lack of sleep and watching people's bodies get blown apart like rag dolls—can all cause PTSD.

PTSD can also happen to anyone who experiences traumatic events, whether in battle or civilian life. Furthermore, there are several risk factors for getting PTSD—length of time of exposure to the trauma (I believe that multiple tours of duty in war zones is a risk factor), how much control the person feels they have during the traumatic event, how isolated the person feels, previous trauma in the person's life, and the presence or lack of a support structure (including society), to name just a few.[12] If soldiers don't have other risk factors, they may come back with horrendous memories that most of the civilian population can never comprehend, but not with emotional damage that rises to the level of PTSD.[13]

In the Civil War, the soldiers who came home with high levels of emotional trauma were said to have "soldier's heart." It is the most poetic term for what we call PTSD, but for me it elicits mixed feelings. Does that mean that the soldiers who didn't come back with severe emotional trauma are heartless?

---

12   http://www.mayoclinic.org/diseases-conditions/post-traumatic-stress-disorder/basics/risk-factors/con-20022540

13   http://www.psychologicalscience.org/news/releases/why-some-soldiers-develop-ptsd-while-others-dont.html#.WDB7B7IrJdh

Random Thought

Cows have no top front teeth, just a *dental pad*. They have bottom front incisors, which they use with the pad and their tongue to pull up grass. The grass gets ground up by the molars in back, swallowed, thrown up back into their mouths (the thrown-up grass is known as "cud"), chewed again, and swallowed again. This goes on all day. Yum.

In *TWD*, the day after the brutal killing of Joe and the Claimers, Rick and Michonne have this conversation:

RICK: Are you okay?
MICHONNE: Yeah.
RICK: I'm okay.
MICHONNE: I know.
RICK: How?
MICHONNE: 'Cause I'm okay, too.

Michonne says she is okay, and certainly her behavior in future episodes shows that she is handling the self-defense necessities of the apocalypse without being debilitated by it. It doesn't make her any better or worse a human being than those characters who are her opposite, like Eugene. She sees the reality, has adapted to it, and doesn't show any severe emotional trauma because of it. Does that mean she is heartless? Is she just a super-human comic book character? I don't think so. I think the way that she copes is part of a range of human responses to battle experiences. Make no mistake—war is hell (as Civil War General William Tecumseh Sherman said), and it can absolutely scar soldiers, mentally, emotionally and physically. But the levels to which it does can vary.

While we absolutely need to do everything we can for soldiers who return with PTSD and lower-level emotional consequences of combat duty, we also need to recognize those soldiers who don't come back with serious emotional trauma. They need to know that they are okay and that if they simply felt that they were doing their duty and come back relatively unscathed, it doesn't mean they are heartless. We need to remember them and acknowledge them, too.

PTSD is a complex topic—as complex as human beings and their lifetime of experiences. It can't be reduced to saying that soldiers come back from war with PTSD because they had to kill, and it can't be used as an argument for total nonviolence, even in self-defense.

The second half of the argument, that we aren't comfortable with killing, is also incomplete. While it is true that the vast majority of us would be horrified at the possibility of being in a situation that would require killing, even for self-defense, this doesn't apply to predators. They have so much rage and need for control that they don't feel any consequences of killing. They don't get PTSD. Predators aren't uncomfortable with killing because they are too closed off; they have sacrificed their feelings of connection with people and live off of their feelings of power over other people's lives.

The argument that people can change is also incomplete. It is true for most people, but again, even in our world, not for predators. With predators operating at will in *TWD*, the top priority is to stop them; whether they can change isn't a concern until that happens. And even if Morgan could capture Negan and keep him in a cell, the odds of change are pretty much zero. The point that Morgan misses is that the predator has to *want* to change. Even in our world, with all the prisons and mental hospitals and with all our counseling, psychiatrists, psychologists, and drugs, we haven't figured out how to get true predators to change. I know of no case, for individual serial killers or murderous leaders, where a change of heart has happened.

Morgan believes that all people can change because he did. He believes the Wolf Leader can change, ties him up in a basement and tells him about everything he learned from Eastman. The Wolf Leader couldn't care less, promises that he will kill everyone in Alexandria if he lives, and takes Denise hostage to get away. But later, he saves Denise from a walker. So, did he change? I don't think so; I think the Wolf Leader just likes Denise.

Denise wins his respect when she talks straight with him and tells him, "You are so full of shit." She also tells him, "You weren't born this way. You changed." And he responds later, "You're right. I changed. And now *I'm gonna help you change.*" (Emphasis mine.) He wants Denise to join the "people don't belong here anymore" program, get a "W" on her forehead and make little baby Wolves. He tells her, "Maybe I want you to stay, since I'm enjoying your company so much." When he saves her, it is about Denise—not about change.

The Wolf Leader was a predator in waiting. The rage and the desire for power and control were already there, kept under wraps by law and society before everything collapsed. I believe the same is true for the Governor and the other *TWD* predators; the seeds were there. Glenn was never going to change into a predator when society collapsed, because the rage wasn't there. It's not in him. Michonne, Carol, Bob, Dale, Tyreese, Sasha, Maggie, Carl, or other Rickites were never going to become predators. Hardened, yes, and with a higher risk of killing for selfish reasons. But not predators.

Random Thought

Sometimes it can be necessary in this world for ordinary people to kill in self-defense, and it can happen without causing insanity or PTSD. What about someone who defends his family and shoots a home invader? What about a woman who manages to overpower and kill her attempted rapist? These people may feel emotional ramifications, but may or may not end up with PTSD. Humans have a vast range of responses to trauma. No one should be blamed for their own emotional response to trauma—whether it is having PTSD or not having it.

It's not in Morgan, either. He didn't seek out or take pleasure in killing, and he wanted to die because he didn't want to keep living with his guilt and dangerous madness. Morgan can't compare his experience with that of an actual predator.

Eastman continues to work with Morgan and gives him a copy of the book, *The Art of Peace*. As Morgan calms down and makes progress, Eastman teaches him aikido. We see them practicing positions (called *forms*), and hear them repeating mantras to each other.

EASTMAN: *To accept everyone.*
MORGAN: *To protect everyone.*
EASTMAN: *And in doing that, protect yourself.*
MORGAN: *To create peace.*

Great Monologues

Lennie James is fabulous as Morgan in his madness phase, living in a self-built fortress and killing anyone who dares to ignore his warning signs. Rick finds him in 512, "Clear," and Lennie brings us the wonderful "I see red" monologue, explaining in rage and grief how his son died.

You gave me the gun. You tried...you tried to get me to do it 'cause I was supposed to do it. I was supposed to kill her, my Jennie. Knew I was supposed to, but I let it go. Let it go like there wasn't gonna be a reckonin'. We was always looking for food, you know? It always came down to food. And I was, I was checking out a cellar and I didn't want Duane to come down there with me and then when I came up, she was standing there right in front of him, and he had his gun up, and he couldn't do it. So I called to him, and he turned, and then she was just...just on him. And I see red, I see red, everything is red, everything that I see is red, and I do it! Finally. Finally was too late.

This one makes me cry every time I see it. Lennie James shoulda gotta Emmy long ago.

Eastman represents a nonviolent utopia. It is a lovely vision—one that may exist on another planet in a galaxy far, far away. And this explains Eastman's view—he lives in an isolated cabin in the woods that is far, far away from the reality of the apocalypse. A few walkers come by—one or two at a time, nothing he can't handle. He kills them before they can get to his goat, Tabitha, then gives them a proper burial. That's the extent of his apocalypse drama. He is a one-man Alexandria, and finding the right cheese recipe from Tabitha's milk is his biggest challenge. He looks perfectly well-fed and says, "I'm not giving up on chocolate anytime soon," for Pete's sake. He can spout nonviolence from his happy vegetarian safe spot, having had no need to act in self-preservation in the face of a walker herd or lawless apocalypse humans.

Eastman's true trauma came before the world went away, and it is when we hear this story that we know Eastman's total nonviolence is a method of coping with his own personal history. He tells Morgan about Crichton Dallas Wilton, a man who escaped from prison and killed Eastman's entire family. After Wilton was back behind bars, Eastman built the cell at his house that he later used to hold Morgan. He captured Wilton from a road crew, brought him there and starved him to death.

Eastman says it took 47 days for Wilton to die, which would have been horrible to watch. Wilton would have been confused and would have demanded to be let out. As days went by without food, he would have asked what the heck was going on. He might have cursed Eastman, begged and apologized for the murders. He would have gotten thinner and weaker, first losing the strength to stand, then to sit, and finally to even move. Can you imagine watching day 39? Day 42? Day 46?

And Eastman clearly gave Crichton Dallas Wilton water, or he would have died within two or three days. Eastman didn't shorten the agony; he stretched it out for each and every one of those 47 days.

Eastman is a good man, like Morgan, so killing someone traumatized him. The devotion to complete nonviolence is his answer, and it heals him, as it does Morgan. But it can't realistically continue beyond the isolated land of Eastman. When faced with a predator, to act on the philosophy of never killing because "all life is precious" puts everyone in danger.

In 516, Morgan meets the Wolf Leader, who is very open about the fact that the Wolves kill people, sometimes entire communities, on a regular basis. Morgan knows that this weird dude with a "W" carved into his forehead is a lethal and continuing threat. But when the Wolf Leader and his partner attack Morgan, he won't kill them. He knocks them out with his aikido life-is-precious peace stick, dumps them into the back of a car and leaves. Then these two and their compatriots go on to wreak havoc in Alexandria.

So here is Morgan's neutrality death toll—the list of those who are killed by the Wolves from the time that Morgan didn't kill the Wolf Leader in 516, to the time Carol does in 609. In memoriam, the people who die because Morgan believes all life is precious are:

- Red Poncho Guy (516)
- Richards, the Alexandrian who was burned by a Molotov cocktail and fell off the wall (602, "JSS")
- Wolf driver of truck that rammed into Alexandria walls (602)
- 11 anonymous Alexandrians (602)
- Holly (602)
- Shelly (602)
- Erin (602)
- Nicholas (603, "Thank You")
- Barnes, part of Glenn and Michonne's team (603)
- Sturgess, part of Glenn and Michonne's team (603)
- Annie, part of Glenn and Michonne's team (603)
- David, husband of Betsy and part of Glenn and Michonne's team (603)
- Betsy, who committed suicide when David didn't return (605)
- 9 anonymous Wolves (602)
- Wolf killed by Carl (602)
- Wolf who says, "People don't belong here" (602)

- "Quick…slow" Wolf (602)
- Wolf killed by Jessie in her house (602)
- Wolf killed by Carol in Olivia's pantry (602)
- 4 anonymous Wolves who attacked Rick in the motor home (603)

Why are Betsy, Nicholas, and the other Alexandrians who were with Glenn and Michonne included? Because when the horn blast from the truck drew half the herd toward it, Glenn and Michonne had to lead their team back to Alexandria, desperate to stay ahead of the herd. They wouldn't have been on that route, they wouldn't have been in that situation if the Wolf hadn't driven the truck into the Alexandria wall.

So the number of neutrality deaths for Morgan is 41. What would Morgan say if someone told him that 41 people would be alive if he had killed the two predator Wolves? Aren't those 41 lives precious?

Also, the tower along the Alexandria wall was weakened when the truck crashed right next to it. Without that, it probably wouldn't have fallen and the walker herd wouldn't have gotten in. So if we include the herd invasion, we can add the deaths of Jessie, Ron, Sam, and other anonymous Alexandrians. Ripples, Morgan. Ripples.

Furthermore, since Morgan knew from the day he met the Wolves that they would continue killing, his neutrality isn't really about "all life is precious." It is about not wanting to get his own hands dirty so that he can keep holding onto his philosophy. He admits as much when he tells Rick, Michonne, and Carol in 607:

All life is precious. And that idea, that idea changed me, it brought me back, and it keeps me living…And I've thought about letting that idea go, but I don't want to.

It's for him, not for other people. He admits that he struggles with it. But for him, at that point, holding onto that philosophy is more important than other people's lives.

And his hands are dirty, whether he likes it or not. Morgan had predators in his custody and he let them go deliberately. I'm not taking responsibility away from the Wolf—his group did the killing, no question. But Morgan also bears partial responsibility for those 41 deaths.

I like Morgan. He is a good man and he was a good father. As a fan, I cheered with happy surprise when he removed his mask at the end of 501. He has had trouble adapting to the reality of the apocalypse, but fortunately, it looks like he will come out of this fog. Morgan broke his own rule with a vengeance in 616, unloading six shots into the man who was about to kill Carol. We can hope Morgan will finally adapt and will join the company of Rickite warriors. Lives will no doubt depend on it.

Death Through Inaction

Sometimes the Rickites encounter someone who is in mortal danger (usually from walkers), and they don't do anything to help. It's a tough call. Deciding whether or not to help requires evaluating within seconds how many fighters and weapons are available, how much time there is, the view of the surrounding area and the number of walkers, and whether it is possible to even make a difference.

In 502, the Rickites see that they can easily handle the number of walkers surrounding a man huddled on top of a large rock (Father Gabriel). But in 416, helping isn't an option. When Rick, Carl and Michonne hear cries for help, Carl runs toward the yells and they see a man surrounded by walkers. Carl raises his gun, but Rick stops him. There are too many walkers, and it is too late, anyway. Before they had a chance to shoot all the walkers, the man would have already been bitten. It is sad, but understandable.

The one death through inaction that is particularly poignant is that of Orange Backpack Guy in 312, "Clear" when Rick, Carl and Michonne are on a run for weapons. As they drive, they see a man with an orange backpack, who yells at them and begs them repeatedly to stop. They don't; they just pass him by. Further on, they have to drive around several broken-down cars and get stuck in the mud on the side of the road. While they are trying to free their car, Orange Backpack Guy comes running around the bend again.

Pleaaasse! Stop!! I'm okay!! I'm begging you!! Pleeaaase!!

He clearly understands the apocalypse "stranger danger" and is doing everything he can to let them know that he is safe. And he does strike us as okay; he sounds very sincere. But our group gets the car out of the mud and drives away.

Rick has too much on his mind at the time, what with planning how to defend the prison against the Governor. He has Carl to protect, he isn't sure yet whether he can trust Michonne, and there is also no clear view to see the number of walkers. If Orange Backpack Guy had come along in a later episode, Rick might have stopped, talked with him a while, and possibly asked the three questions.

On the way back, Rick, Carl, and Michonne spot something on the side of the road—mostly eaten human remains and an orange backpack.

They take the orange backpack with them, and it reappears several times in the show. Which makes sense—it is a very useful item. Carl packs it in 403 when he has to move into the administration building during the flu outbreak, Glenn uses it when he leaves the prison with

Great Directing and Cinematography

One thing that makes the Orange Backpack Guy story so memorable is what happens after his death. After they pass the remains, the car slowly backs up to the backpack and stops. In a great shot, the camera is on the other side of the road and aimed level with the car. Through the car windows we see the far back door open, and through the space underneath the car we see the backpack being picked up. This is their world. "Sorry we couldn't save you Orange Backpack Guy, but now we need your stuff." (My quote, not theirs.)

Tara, and Rick spots it at Terminus. The orange backpack makes it out of Terminus (somehow), and Daryl wears it in 614, "Twice as Far."

Killing through inaction is always sad, and not just for the person who dies. It is also sad for the Rickites or other good people who have to stand by and watch a person die. In 616, the Saviors hang the Last Librarian from a large chain over a bridge. Aaron wants to try to shoot the chain apart to save him; but the links are too strong and the Rickites can't waste their bullets on a target that would take expert aim. As they watch the Last Librarian choke to death, their faces reflect horror and anger at their helplessness.

I'm an optimist about most of humanity. I think that most of us want to help if we can. We want to take action, make things better, and stop the bullies. When we can't, it hurts.

Killing Them Not So Softly—Rick and Carol

All the killing that Rick or Carol have done so far is justified. Period. Rick and Carol kill in self-defense. They do get more hardened about the killing they have to do, but neither of them is too far gone, because they have not killed for selfish reasons or as predators. To show this, here are the lists of kills for both Rick and Carol, up through the end of Season 6.

Rick

Season 1: 0

Season 2: 3
• Dave and Tony in the bar. Dave reached for his gun. Self-defense.
• Shane. Shane lured Rick into the woods to kill him. Self-defense.

Season 3: 4
• Tomas, one of the surviving prisoners. Tomas tries to shoot Rick and pushes a walker onto him. Self-defense.
• 3 Woodbury Fighters during the rescue of Glenn and Maggie. Battle situation.

Season 4: 4

- Lou, a member of the Claimers. Rick is trying to find a way to hide and get away from these guys, goes into a bathroom and finds Lou. They fight, Lou goes for his gun and Rick strangles him. Self-defense.

- Joe, the leader of the Claimers. Rick tears out Joe's jugular with his teeth after Joe states that they will kill Daryl and Rick and rape Michonne and Carl. Self-defense.

- Dan, the member of the Claimers who attacked Carl. Rick stabs him repeatedly and rips the knife up through his chest. Not exactly self-defense, since Dan had already dropped his knife. But does anyone believe that Dan hadn't done this before, or wouldn't do it again? And what are they going to do, call the cops? It was execution without a trial, because everyone saw what Dan did.

- Alex, Gareth's brother at Terminus. Rick shoots Alex after Gareth gives a hand signal and his people start shooting the Rickites. Self-defense and battle situation.

Season 5: 12

- Baseball Bat Guy at Terminus butchering trough. Self-defense.

- Throat Slitting Guy at Terminus butchering trough. Self-defense.

- 5 Unnamed Terminus fighters. Self-defense and battling out of the compound.

- Mike, Terminus member at Father Gabriel's church. Self-defense.

- Albert, Terminus member at Father Gabriel's church. Self-defense.

- Gareth, Terminus leader at Father Gabriel's church. Definitely self-defense. Just ask Bob.

- Bob Lamson, the cop at Grady Memorial Hospital. Rick runs into him with his car and then shoots him during the Beth and Carol rescue mission. Battle situation.

- Pete, the drinking, porch-smoking, Alexandrian surgeon/wife-beater/murderer of Reggie. Rick comes close to killing Pete for selfish reasons, but he resists this temptation. When Rick does shoot

Pete in 516, it is the result of the fastest trial in history. Pete comes into the community meeting with a sword, slices Reggie's throat, Abraham grabs Pete and holds him down, Reggie dies in Deanna's arms, a crying Deanna acts as witness, judge and jury and tells Rick, "Do it," and Rick shoots Pete. All in the span of 57 seconds.

Season 6: 11

- 5 Unnamed Wolves who attack Rick in the RV. Self-defense.
- Ethan, Hilltop Community member who stabs their leader, Gregory, and then attacks Rick. Self-defense.
- 5 Saviors in the satellite compound. Proactive self-defense battle situation.

Rick's kill total is 34, and none of them are predatory or done for selfish reasons. None.

Carol

Season 1: 0

Season 2: 0

Season 3: 0

Season 4: 3

- Karen and David. This was misguided pro-active self-defense. More on this special case later.
- Lizzie. Tragic, but still proactive self-defense.

Season 5: 13

- 5 Unnamed Terminus fighters/residents. Self-defense and battle situation.
- Mary, Gareth's mother. Self-defense and battle situation.
- 7 Unnamed Wolves during the Wolf attack on Alexandria. Self-defense and defense of the Alexandrians.

Season 6: 8

- Wolf Leader during herd invasion of Alexandria. Self-defense.

- Donnie, Savior who kidnapped Maggie and Carol. Self-defense.
- Michelle, Savior who kidnapped Maggie and Carol. Self-defense.
- Paula, Savior who kidnapped Maggie and Carol. Self-defense.

NOTE: At this point Carol leaves Alexandria so she won't have to kill for those she loves.

- Miles, one of the Saviors who threatens her on the road. Self-defense.
- Jiro, one of the Saviors who threatens her on the road. Self-defense.
- 2 Unnamed Saviors who threaten her on the road. Self-defense.

Carol's total kill count is 24, and none of them are predatory. It's also significant that Rick and Carol have killed fewer people than the predators do during Andrea and Morgan's neutrality time:

Andrea/The Governor 50
Morgan/The Wolves 41
Rick 34
Carol 24

Furthermore, it takes Rick and Carol six seasons to get to their totals. The Governor's 50 neutrality-time kills run from episodes 315 to 408, less than one season. And the Wolf 41 neutrality-time kills happen from 516 to 609, also considerably less than a full season. This means the predator kill rate is at least six times higher than that of the people who kill only when they are forced to.

Make no mistake, Rick is at risk of crossing the line. He is tempted to kill both Pete and Carter in Alexandria, and he entertains the idea of killing Alexandrians one by one until they hand over the town leadership to the Rickites. He hasn't killed innocent people yet, but he can see it from where he is standing.

Brutality vs. Predation

Even though the Rickites have not killed innocent people, they have committed brutal acts. Rick is brutal when he kills Joe and Dan. Even Daryl tries to separate Rick as a person from this act.

DARYL: *Hey, what you did last night? Anybody would have done that.*
RICK: *No, not that.*
DARYL: *Somethin' happened. That ain't you.*
RICK: *Daryl, you saw what I did to Tyreese. It ain't all of it, but that's me. That's why I'm here now, that's why Carl is.*

Rick and some others in the group have become ruthless in defending themselves and those they love. But being brutal doesn't make you a predator. It's the difference between the *how* of killing, which in this case is brutally; and the *why* of killing, which in this case is self-defense.

When Sasha, Rick, Abraham, and Michonne kill the Terminians in St. Sarah's church, it is brutal. The level of stabbing and head bashing goes far beyond what is necessary to kill the cannibals. The Rickites who aren't taking part—Glenn, Tyreese, Maggie, and Tara—look on in shock, and even the killers themselves need to justify the scene they have created.

RICK: *It could have been us.*
SASHA: *(after a long pause) Yeah.*

So why are the Rickites becoming more brutal? The brutality of Joe's death was born of necessity; Rick had no weapons and Joe held him in such a position that his teeth were all he could use. But the brutality of the deaths of Dan and the Terminians stems from another source: rage. Not only at the Claimers and Terminians, but at the Governor, at the walkers, at everything they have been through. The Rickites have built up rage and deep, deep grief at every awful thing they have to deal with every day, at every loss of someone they loved. For some of them, this rage is a factor that threatens to overwhelm them, to greater or lesser degrees.

The Rickites have been very good at reminding each other not to let go of who they were. Glenn does this at Terminus in 501 when he insists that they take the time to release other imprisoned people, saying "That's still who we are. It's gotta be." But even Glenn, arguably the most positive and peaceful member of the group, admits to sliding down a path toward not caring. In 509, after Terminus, after Bob, after

Random Thought

Rick is right. When the Terminians enter St. Sarah's, Gareth offers to let Father Gabriel leave with Judith, but changes his mind when Judith starts to cry and reveals the hiding place. "I don't know, maybe we'll keep the kid. I'm starting to like this girl." The Terminians don't see baby Judith as a little symbol of hope for the future. They see her as veal.

losing Beth, he says about Terminus, "If it were now, I wouldn't make us stop. We'd run right by."

Living in a constantly violent world, the Rickites need to find ways to vent their anger, to channel it, to remember their values, and to find moments of peace. Michonne understands this, and it is after hearing Glenn's admission that she insists they need to find a place to call home, because, "You can be out here too long."

Too much rage will eventually spill over if there is no break from the trauma or a chance to vent. How much it takes depends on the individual—I don't think any amount of anger would lead Glenn to kill an innocent person. But Rick has come close, and Daryl tells Carol that he should have killed Dwight in the woods, even though Dwight was never threatening his life.

They are not in danger of becoming predators; but they are in danger of losing their caring about other people, and could end up thinking only of personal survival and killing callously and for selfish reasons.

I hope all the bearers of light are watching over them, and that we will never see that happen.

Carol Killing Karen and David

Carol killed Karen and David in an outright panic, and she experienced that panic because of her relationship with children and her strong instincts as a mom.

Carol lost her own daughter, Sophia, to a walker attack. So when the Rickites settle in at the prison, she teaches the children how to protect themselves. She conducts story time for the kids, and inserts secret lessons in proper knife-wielding. It is a way to make up for not being there for Sophia.

Her feelings of responsibility weigh even heavier when in 402, "Infected," a dying father asks her to take care of his children—Lizzie and Mika—"like they're yours." She agrees, so now she has her own adopted apocalypse children to protect. It is very shortly after this that she learns Karen and David have the flu. When Carol kills them, it is a panicked attempt to save not just the community in general, but her own children. She needed to stop the flu from spreading—to Lizzie and Mika. She's a mom.

The problem with her logic is that flu victims can be contagious before there are any symptoms. Karen and David had already been in contact with any number of people. Besides that, they were both already quarantined before Carol killed them, so that stopped any further spread anyway.

But Carol panics, and this blocks any clear thinking. As Aaron says, "Fear shrinks the brain." (513, "Forget") Would Carol have had the same reaction if she didn't have responsibility for Lizzie and Mika? Perhaps. But killing Karen and David was an emotional reaction that made no logical sense. If Carol had been thinking clearly, I think she would have recognized this.

Shane Killing Otis

While trying to get away from the high school FEMA shelter with a respirator for Carl's operation, Shane shoots Otis in the leg so the walkers chasing them both will stop and chow down on Otis, allowing

Shane to get away. It was a cold move, and it was in fact murder. But in defense of Shane (just a little bit), his options were fairly limited.

As with Carol, previous events fed into Shane's decision. After Otis accidentally shot Carl, Rick ran with Carl in his arms to Hershel's farm, and Shane ran with Otis. Otis started slowing down, because he is very heavy and couldn't run that far. He told Rick the direction to go and stopped to catch his breath. Long before they are at the FEMA shelter, Shane knows Otis's physical limitations.

As they are trying to get away from the high school, Otis is again slowed due to his weight, and Shane is slowed down due to an ankle injury. Neither of them can outrun the crowd of walkers following them, and they are almost out of ammunition. If they both die, then Carl also dies. Shane could have sacrificed himself to the walkers, but he knows that Otis can't run that fast and would probably also be killed. He probably figured he would be faster than Otis, even with a bad ankle. Or it could have been simple survival—if it was a choice between him or Otis dying, it was going to be Otis.

To see what else Shane could have done, we can think of how Rick might have handled the same situation. Rick certainly would have done anything to get the respirator back for Carl, and possibly with the same result—Otis dead and Rick returning to the farm. But I think Rick would have approached it differently—he would have talked to Otis.

Rick would have proposed a plan and at least let Otis buy into it. Like Shane, he would have known that he was in better physical condition than Otis, even with a twisted ankle. He could have suggested that Otis give him the backpack with the respirator and that he would run ahead for the car, then bring the car back to get Otis. This would also leave Otis free to move more quickly without the heavy load.

I think that Otis would have agreed to this plan. He was a good person who felt responsibility for what happened to Carl. It might not have worked—the walkers might have gotten to Otis anyway. But at least he would have been included in the decision; at least Rick would have honored him as a human being enough to let him agree to the risk. It would have been tragic, but not cold. And Rick could have honestly told Otis' wife Patricia the truth about what happened.

Shane's killing of Otis was very much in line with his approach to the apocalypse; that only the strong are going to survive, so it isn't worth spending time and energy trying to save those who are weak and are a drain on the group, anyway. It is selfish at its core, and the selfishness was always there. All the apocalypse did was enhance who Shane was to begin with, and who he was to begin with made it easier for him to kill Otis.

4

The 'Why' of Fighting

You're not the good guys. You should know that.
–Michelle, 613, "The Same Boat"

Michelle's statement above is wrong. She is operating on a principle that says, "Your people killed my people, my people killed your people—it's all the same." Morgan also has this view, and other Rickites are starting to have doubts about their own battle efforts. When Tara goes on the mission to attack the Savior compound in 612, she tells Father Gabriel that she lied to Denise to cover up the fact "That I'd done something like this before. That I didn't like it." She is equating the attack on the Savior compound with the Governor's final attack on the prison.

So it's all the same, right? In a word—no. It's not the same. As we cheer when the Rickites defeat their foes, we know in our guts the lesson that has been trained out of our brains: the *why* of fighting is crucial. The Rickites themselves know that the *why* matters; it is part of how they screen whether to bring somebody into the group. When they ask someone why they killed people, an answer resembling, "Because I wanted their stuff" would probably not encourage them to accept the person into the Rickite circle.

Ideals matter. The rules by which a community operates matter. The levels of desire for power or willingness to relinquish it in a society's leaders will determine how likely that society is to both attack other communities and to kill and oppress its own people. And as ideals go, comparing the Rickite society with most other *TWD* communities,

Rick and his people are on the side of good. Not angelic and hardly perfect, but definitely good.

As fans, our response to Carol's decision to stop fighting shows that we know this; and that we still know, inside, the importance of the *why* of fighting.

When Carol becomes horrified at the number of people she has killed, we are glad that she hasn't become too hardened. We certainly don't want her to be like Paula, her nemesis in 613 who says, "I stopped counting when I hit double digits; that's right around the time I stopped feeling bad about it."

But while we sympathize with Carol's feelings, we don't really like her newfound pacifism. Our hearts sink a little as she leaves Alexandria, and we are relieved when we realize she sewed an automatic rifle into a large jacket sleeve before going. When she uses it on the men who try to assault her on the road, we aren't disappointed—far from it. We

Great Writing

We need to see the humanity and relationship stuff, too. If we didn't care about these characters, it wouldn't matter to us when they get into trouble or die. We want to see Carol and Daryl's loving banter, we want to see Bob helping Sasha out of her fear, and we want to see Carl score 112 ounces of chocolate pudding. We want to see the group chuckle at the prison when they realize that Maggie and Glenn are alone in the guard tower—again. We want to see Rick bringing mints to Michonne when he can't find toothpaste, and we want to see Denise kiss Tara and tell her that "being afraid sucks." We want to see our much-loved characters as real people, not just interchangeable, two-dimensional, generic zombie-fighting apocalypse inhabitants. The writers accomplish this with skill, which is one of the reasons that the show is so popular.

happily agree with Rick when he finds what is left of her attackers. "I'm proud of her. ...That woman, she's a force of nature."

Do we want Carol to keep killing because we love her and don't want to see her hurt? Absolutely. But if that's all there is to it, then why aren't we content to see her bake cookies and find happiness with Tobin? Are we bloodthirsty? Is our action addiction only satisfied by watching her repel invasions and make things go boom? To a degree, yes. *TWD* brings us a world in which people are fighting for their lives, and giving Carol no greater troubles than running out of beets and chocolate bars would go against the grain of the show. Paraphrasing Carol herself, "You can bake cookies, but you can't *just* bake cookies."

But it's not just that. It's the knowledge that when Carol kills (except for the panicked mistake with Karen and David), her *why* for killing is valid. It goes beyond defending herself and those she loves, because the Saviors could do that. Paula could do that. We cheer when Carol kills the men on the road, after her promise not to kill, because she is Carol, the Saviors are the Saviors, and they are looking for innocent people to hurt. She is not only saving herself, she is stopping them. And that is why we cheer.

Imagine if Carol left Alexandria with an automatic rifle up her sleeve and used it on a father and son who looked emaciated and did nothing more than helplessly ask her for food. We wouldn't cheer; we would be shocked. We would wonder if she had gone slightly crazy like Morgan did. When Carol killed Lizzie, we didn't cheer. Lizzie was dangerous, but not deliberately so, and our response is sadness about that tragedy. It was a valid *why*, and we understood Carol's decision. But our cheers happen when the *why* involves taking out bad people who are intent on harming others. Our instincts are right.

In 609, "No Way Out," Rick tells an unconscious Carl that he wants to show him the New World; but Rick doesn't have it quite right. This isn't the New World, it's the Transitional World, and who prevails in the struggle during the transition matters very much. The New World could wind up being run by Negan, which wouldn't be much of a world worth living in, and which would actually lead to more deaths than a war that stopped him. In *TWD*, predator leaders cause more deaths than leaders of democracies, and these fictional statistics that come from a television show are backed up by actual historical numbers in our world.

Dr. R.J. Rummel, a professor of political science at the University of Hawaii, spent his entire career studying and compiling the statistics of war deaths and murder by governments of their own citizens or citizens under their care. He began his research as an undergraduate, and states in his book, *Power Kills: Democracy as a Method of Nonviolence*, that his true interest was "in understanding and doing something about the legal killing called war."[14]

After years of study, he didn't end up promoting globalization, pacifism, internationalism, or moral equivalency among nations. He didn't conclude that war will be ended through arms control, eliminating poverty (he accounted for wealth in his studies), promoting understanding, or practicing artful diplomacy and effective crisis management. These are all good efforts to pursue, but after extensive and in-depth research, Rummel came to a position that was a surprise even to him: democracies are the least warlike and the least likely to murder their own people. Democracy is a path to peace.

Rummel examined deaths both from war and from *democide*, which is a term he coined that includes three forms of government murder:

Genocide—murder based on race or ethnicity (think Adolf Hitler)
Politicide—the murder of political opponents (think Josef Stalin)
Mass Murder—random murder to accomplish a goal or instill fear (think Mao Tse-tung)

Rummel examined over 8,200 documents—human rights reports, studies, journal articles and news stories—covering democide. He found that in the years 1900-1987, over 169 million people were

---

14   R.J. Rummel, *Power Kills: Democracy as a Method of Nonviolence* (Transaction Publishers, 1997), ix

murdered by totalitarian regimes. The Soviet Union killed almost 70 million people from 1917-1987; Nazi Germany killed over 20 million people from 1933-1945; and the People's Republic of China under Mao Tse-tung killed over 35 million people from 1949-1987. Other less well-known dictators also contributed to the 169 million total.[15]

In contrast, from 1900-1987, the number of deaths from all the wars around the globe, both international and civil, is 38 million.[16] Democide caused more than four times more deaths than war did. Rulers with the most absolute power over people's lives also kill the most people.

In addition, democracies do not wage war against each other. In his book, Rummel quotes a 1964 study by Dean Babst, which found that "for 116 major wars of 438 countries from 1789 to 1941, not one war involved democracies on opposite sides."[17] Babst also found that ten democracies participated in World War I, and none fought against each other; and fourteen democracies participated in World War II, with none fighting against each other. Finally, Babst looked at wars after 1945, and still found no democracies on opposite sides.[18] So from 1789-1964, no democracies have waged war against each other. None. Zip. Nada.

Why is this the case? Rummel offers not just statistics, but reasons. One reason is that libertarian democracies (a term that doesn't include countries that are political democracies, technically, but don't have many civil rights for citizens) routinely use negotiation and compromise as methods for resolving internal conflict, so negotiation and compromise are the natural and preferred methods to solve international conflict. Also, in libertarian democracies, freedom of speech allows all individuals and groups to voice their opinions, so opponents of war can freely, safely and publicly bring up their arguments. Finally, most people don't

---

15 Rummel, *Power Kills: Democracy as a Method of Nonviolence*, 94

16 Rummel, *Power Kills: Democracy as a Method of Nonviolence*, 92

17 Rummel, *Power Kills: Democracy as a Method of Nonviolence*, 26

18 Rummel, *Power Kills: Democracy as a Method of Nonviolence*, 26

want to go to war, and in a democracy they have a say. On this point, Rummel quotes philosopher Immanuel Kant's book, *Perpetual Peace*:

> [If] the consent of the citizens is required in order to decide that war should be declared...nothing is more natural than that they would be very cautious in commencing such a poor game, decreeing for themselves all the calamities of war.[19]

War must absolutely be the last resort. It is good to try negotiations, blockades, sanctions, or other diplomatic efforts, if possible, prior to the use of military force. But if these methods don't get the desired results, the opposing country or group is continuing to be predatory and aggressive, or if an attack requires a prompt and strong reactive self-defense response, then military action is a tool that must not be left in the toolbox out of fear, distaste, or wanting to hold onto a Morgan-like neutrality. It would be nice if we could all live in a goat-filled vegetarian safe spot, but we don't. Our world is tougher than that, and we need the people who are fighting for positive principles to do just that. Smartly, intelligently, and not out of ego or revenge, but definitely in a way that is daring and firm. Because letting the bullies win—letting Negan win—will never, ever, ever make the world a better place or make it truly peaceful.

Each individual has to decide what parameters matter to them when weighing whether to support a military effort. Here are some that I created for myself:

1. We (or our allies) have been attacked. This one stands on its own.
2. The opposing group or country are predators. If another country is hostile or has different philosophies, but isn't aggressive or predatory, declaring war may not be the right decision. This is a tough one, because other countries may be committing mass democide and brutally oppressing their own people. But if they aren't attacking other countries or indicating that they intend to

---

19 Rummel, *Power Kills: Democracy as a Method of Nonviolence*, 104

do so, the people of a democracy will probably not support a war against them. At least not for very long.

3. The consequences of not going to war must be worse than having our own citizens injured or killed in battle. This is important. Whatever the other country or group is doing must be so horrible that stopping it is worth our own fathers, sons, brothers, sisters, husbands, daughters, mothers, wives and friends coming back wounded in body and mind, or not coming back at all. We must be able to justify that sacrifice to our soldiers and their families.

Once these parameters have been met, there is a valid *why* for fighting, and the decision to go to war has been made, then war should be fought to be won. Starting a war and planning the exit is like getting married and planning the divorce; it puts a damper on strong efforts to make it work. Facing a half-hearted effort, the predators will go on as they have, pleased that they don't have any truly dedicated opposition. They will simply wait for the exit, and people will continue to suffer.

The Rickites kill only when it's truly necessary, and their reasons are valid. Because of that, it is very important for them to fight hard once the decision is made. After deciding to fight, the Rickites and their allies need to go forth with confidence. They need to know that they are acting in self-defense and in defense of the positive principles that they practice. They need to be strong in who they are as a community and proud of who they are as a community. They have to know that they are fighting for the right reasons—that the sacrifice that will undoubtedly be made is worth it. The *why* is crucial.

5

Principles Worth Fighting For

"I couldn't sacrifice one of us for the greater good because… because we are the greater good. We're the reason we're still here, not me."
–Rick, 315, "This Sorrowful Life"

So what are the principles of the Rickites? What are they defending, beyond their own turf and their own people? What are the ideas that Rick, Daryl, Michonne, Carl, Maggie, Glenn, Abraham, Rosita, Eugene, Tara, Father Gabriel and all the Rickites live by that are worth fighting for?

Here is a list of positive traits for our democratic leader and his group. It is not inclusive of all the positive traits for a society in our world, because the *TWD* world hasn't advanced enough to include principles, for instance, like not putting someone on trial twice for the same offense. So this is a list of the principles that the Rickites have had a chance to demonstrate so far.

Caring About Other People, Not Just Your Group

How many walkers have you killed? How many people have you killed? Why?
–The questions asked to potential new members of the Rickites group.

Rick brings other people into his group. He takes risks for strangers. It is a view that is expansive, positive, and faith-filled, and it is one of the traits that separates him from Shane. Shane is not a predator, but he is self-centered. His focus is on keeping his own group alive rather than helping others, and he is willing to give up on people quickly.

When Rick wants to return to Atlanta to save Merle, Shane argues against it. When Rick sends people out to look for Sophia, Shane opposes that as well. Shane's instinct is to pull in and stay safe, showing an underlying view that risks are too dangerous. Rick's instinct is to reach out and trust that strength will be there, showing an underlying view that risks will bring rewards.

Rick establishes this trait of caring for others early in the show. In 104, "Vatos," when Rick, T-Dog, Glenn and Daryl return to Atlanta to save Merle and retrieve a lost bag of guns, Glenn is kidnapped by another group. The Rickites capture a member of the other group and go to negotiate a hostage exchange. The group's leader, Guillermo, agrees to the exchange, but only if the Rickites also turn over the bag of guns.

Rick's group goes back to the building where they hid the guns and debates what to do. Daryl and T-Dog express doubts about the plan—the risk is trusting Guillermo, bringing him the guns, and getting killed anyway. The alternative is to take the guns back home and leave Glenn behind. But Rick is firm.

> T-DOG: *The question is, do you trust that man's word?*
> DARYL: *No, the question is what you're willing to bet on it. Could be more than them guns; it could be your life. Is Glenn worth that to you?*
> RICK: *What life I have I owe to him. I was nobody to Glenn—just some idiot stuck in a tank. He could have walked away, but he didn't. Neither will I.*

Rick also shows his understanding that it takes strength to survive. He'll bring the guns—loaded and ready for battle. As a good leader, Rick owns this decision and doesn't ask the others to take the risk with him; he tells T-Dog and Daryl to go to back to camp. They refuse, and a small military group is born for the best of reasons: to save a man who was a total stranger a month ago.

In another example, Rick shows caring for others in the middle of the final confrontation with the Terminians at St. Sarah's. When Gareth offers to leave the Rickites alone and never cross their path again, Rick quotes Gareth's statement to Bob back to him, "But you'll cross someone's path. You'd 'do this to anyone,' right?"

Rick is not just saving his own group; he is stopping the reign of the cannibals and saving future victims. And he knows it.

After the Governor's second attack, Rick brings the ragtag remnants of the fallen Woodbury community back to the prison. All of Woodbury's able-bodied people were at the battle (and then killed), so most of those left behind are old, sick, or children. They will not be able to contribute in strength, but clearly Rick doesn't care about that. They need a place, and he trusts that they will find a way to help build the prison community.

The Rickites continue to welcome others. Glenn and Daryl meet Bob on the road and bring him back. And when we learn that Karen has the flu, she says that "David from the Decatur group" is also sick, so we know they brought in survivors from Decatur, Georgia. The Rickites reach out carefully, vetting their prospects with the three questions. But their lives are stable at this point and they want to build a real home at the prison, both for themselves and for others. That is the nature of the Rickites. That's how they roll.

In the best example, Rick takes the entire community of Alexandria under his wing. It's not an easy journey for him, because he doesn't trust their ability to defend themselves, and they don't trust him, either. But as the Alexandrians learn about the true dangers outside their walls, they step up to the challenge, bit by bit.

Rick, in turn, accepts them as his adopted community, bit by bit, and the Alexandrians prove themselves in the wonderful premiere episode of the back half of Season 6, "No Way Out," in which nearly the entire population of Alexandria follows Rick's lead, faces their fears and defeats the invading walker herd alongside the Rickites.

Rick's expansiveness goes on to include alliances with other communities, with Maggie forging agreements with the Hilltop Community leader. Negan presents the greatest threat to a peaceful and free New World. But when good people join together with all their might, they can move mountains. Even a mountain of Saviors.

Understanding That the Group Rules, Not You

What I said last year, that first night after the farm, it can't be like that. It can't.
–Rick, 315, "This Sorrowful Life"

The Rickites go back and forth on democracy, but always return to it when they are settled. At the end of Season 2, the group is forced off the farm, cars run out of gas, and night is approaching with a herd of walkers nearby. Some terrified members of the group do not yet trust

Great Monologues

Rick's exhausted, angry, intense speech naming himself as leader is one of Andrew Lincoln's (many) greatest hits.

I say there's a place for us but maybe, maybe it's just another pipe dream, maybe I'm fooling myself again. Why don't you go and find out yourself? Send me a postcard! Go on, there's the door. You can do better, let's see how far you get. No takers? Fine, but get one thing straight. You're staying—this isn't a democracy anymore.

Comparing this speech with the "he talked about the deer" speech shows the range, depth and commitment of Andrew's acting. And it doesn't stop there. All of Andrew's monologues have different tones, styles and emotional notes, and all are completely matched with the group's situation. Again—yet again—shoulda gotta Emmy.

Rick to get them through that first night, and they debate splitting off and going their own ways. Rick knows that separating is the most dangerous thing for everyone, so he stops this from happening by taking over leadership of the group and starting the era of Ricktatorship.

Rick is right at this point. While they are on the road and fighting for survival, a military-type hierarchy is necessary. There simply isn't time to sit around, form councils, debate and vote on how to proceed; someone has to give orders and have them followed immediately. Hopefully that person has the knowledge and skills to fight successfully, the wisdom to listen to his or her advisors, and the trust to let others make decisions when they are on their own in the field. Rick demonstrates all these qualities, but his word is final as long as they are on the road.

Once the Rickites are living in the prison, there is more security—until they are faced with attacks from the Governor. When Rick and the Governor meet face to face in 313, "Arrow in the Doorpost," Rick is confronted with the dark side of total control, both in how the Governor operates and in what he asks Rick to do. The Governor tells Rick that if he will hand over Michonne (who stabbed the Governor in the eye), Woodbury will stop threatening the prison.

At first, Rick doesn't tell the group about this Faustian bargain; but he can't stand holding back from his people. When he decides not to turn over Michonne, he knows the Governor will attack and that the Rickites will have to choose whether to fight or flee. In 315, in another of Andrew Lincoln's great monologues, he brings this choice to the group:

> *What we do, what we're willing to do, who we are—it's not my call. It can't be. … We're the reason we're still here, not me. This is life and death. How you live…how you die…it isn't up to me. I'm not your Governor. We choose to go. We choose to stay. We stick together. We vote.*

The decision is everyone's. The group chooses to stay and fight, the Governor's 2nd attack is repelled, and they have a stable community for a brief time. It is now that Rick completely releases his hold on power (a choice that a predator leader would never make), a council is formed to weigh decisions for the community, and Rick becomes just one of the general population. Their stability and security allows this and brings other benefits: prosperity, education for children, and the ability to plan for the future.

In 502, after the group escapes Terminus, they are on the move again in a survival situation. They morph easily back into military mode, roaming the forest with guns at the ready, and Rick again makes final decisions—sort of. When Abraham wants to convince the Rickites to join him in his quest to reach DC, he knows that it is Rick's nod of approval he needs. But by Season 5, it is a quasi-Ricktatorship and Rick doesn't control the decisions of individuals. When Glenn tells Abraham that he and Maggie will go to DC if Abraham stays long enough to help capture the Terminians, Rick objects. But Glenn tells him flatly, "It's not your call." And he and Maggie do go with Abraham.

No other *TWD* leader honors democracy like Rick. Not even Deanna, who in some ways is the worst kind of dictator. She is a wolf in sheep's clothing, and underneath the dinner parties and smiles, she calls all the shots. In a world where people must defend their very lives on a daily basis, she doesn't allow Alexandrians to have guns. She tells everyone what job they will have, and she even admits to Rick the political conditions under her rule.

> RICK: *Everybody said you gave them jobs.*
> DEANNA: *Mm-hm. Yeah. Part of this place. Looks like the communists won after all.*

After Rick fights Pete and waves a gun in the air, Deanna sets up a community meeting to discuss whether to exile Rick. Maggie, developing her leadership skills, confronts her about this idea.

> MAGGIE: *You let all of us in. You talked to us. You decided. And now you want to put that decision on a group of very frightened people who might not have the whole story. That's not leadership.*
> REGGIE: *Tonight is, is just a forum. It's just for people to say their piece.*
> DEANNA: *And I'll make the decision, as I've done since the beginning.*

Great Monologues

Rick's speeches are almost never about personal issues. In contrast, Lori's monologue to Carl before she dies is personal. Carl's "I'd be fine if you died" monologue to his father is personal. Morgan's "I see red" speech is personal. Father Gabriel's "I always lock the doors at night" is a personal confession. But with the exception of Rick's personal "You are not safe" and "He talked about the deer" speeches (one to and the other about Carl), his monologues are to the group. From "This isn't a democracy anymore," to "I'm not your Governor," to "We all can change," to "We are the walking dead," to the "You're going to change" speech to the Alexandrians, Rick's monologues come from his position as leader. He speaks to and for the group. Any great leader leads and yet also embodies the outlook and needs of the people. Andrew Lincoln and the writers have brought this to us beautifully. (Shoulda gotta…you know.)

Poor Maggie. She innocently assumed that Deanna was going to put the decision to a vote. Maggie's astute point is about the importance of giving people all the facts before asking them to make a decision. It never occurred to her that the community meeting was just a way for Deanna to claim support for a decision she intended to dictate all along.

Rick is not exiled, and in Season 6, there is brief stability in Alexandria after the walker herd is defeated. Deanna is bitten during the invasion and dies, and Rick becomes leader of Alexandria. When the Rickites learn about the Saviors, Rick again brings the decision of whether or not to fight to the group. As long as they are in a stable home behind walls, the Rickites and those they adopt move back to democracy, and Rick is willing to abdicate power.

Letting Others Make the Decision

You know what you know, and you're sure of it. But I'm not.
–Michonne to Rick, 511, "The Distance"

From the beginning, Rick recognizes ability and listens to ideas, no matter who offers them. He instinctively operates on the principle that many heads make better plans, which is one sign of a good leader.

In 102, "Guts," Rick, Glenn, T-Dog, Jacqui, Morales and Andrea are trapped in a department store with walkers pressing against the glass doors. Rick has just met these people; he is not yet their leader.

As they try to figure out an escape through the sewers, Jacqui says that the sewers might be accessible from the building basement. Glenn has a plan for exploring the basement tunnels, but hesitates when Andrea objects. Rick encourages him, saying, "Speak your mind." Glenn says he will go into the sewers and gives assignments to everyone else, with good reasons for each choice. Rick naturally and easily moves into a leadership role; not by insisting on his own plan, but by acknowledging Glenn's. He claps Glenn on the shoulder, saying, "Okay. Everybody knows their jobs." He listens to this capable advisor.

The escape through the tunnels doesn't work, and Rick comes up with another idea. Because he has listened to others, trust has been built and they are willing to listen to him. His plan leads to the marvelous sequence in "Guts" where Rick and Glenn put on protective coats, chop up a downed walker, smear blood and guts all over themselves and make their way safely through the walker-infested streets of Atlanta.

In 507, Rick agrees to a plan that goes against his own instincts. The group discusses a rescue to get Beth and Carol out of Grady Memorial Hospital. Rick wants to go in, kill the cops who guard the hospital, and take Beth and Carol by force. Tyreese speaks up with another plan: they should kidnap two of the hospital guards, then offer a prisoner exchange. This way, "Everybody goes home."

Rick doesn't like it. He insists that his plan is more sure to work. But Daryl supports Tyreese's alternative, and Rick accepts the advice of the two other men. They go with the prisoner exchange, and it works—to a degree. Three people do die, but two of the deaths happen only because Dawn scuttles the deal at the last minute. The point is that Rick listened to his people. In a military situation, the decision was his; but he was willing to take advice from others, even when it wasn't his preference.

In 511, the Rickites are staying in a barn and trying to decide whether to trust clean-cut Aaron, who makes broken music boxes come to life and hates applesauce, and who invites them to Alexandria. On the decision of whether to go with Aaron, Rick's leadership is challenged even more directly.

After the horrors of Woodbury and Terminus, Rick wants no part of going with this stranger to another unknown community. He would rather stay on the road with his own, trusted group. This time, it is Michonne who disagrees with him. She listens to her gut, and believes that Aaron is sincere. She senses that the Rickites desperately need a safe place; they are in danger of being on the road for too long and becoming "too far gone." She wants to see if Alexandria is a decent place, but Rick objects:

> RICK: *Your way is dangerous. Mine isn't.*
> MICHONNE: *Passing up someplace where we can live? Where Judith can live? That's pretty dangerous.*

Rick agrees to test the truth of Aaron's story of how he found them and that he has a car and an RV about five miles away. A scouting party finds the vehicles where Aaron said they would be and reports this back to the group, but Rick says he still hasn't decided.

> CARL: *What do you mean? Why wouldn't we go?*
> MICHONNE: *If he were lying, or if he wanted to hurt us. But he isn't, and he doesn't. We need this. So we're going. All of us. Somebody say something if they feel differently.*

Michonne gives this speech to the group; she is not consulting Rick. She has spoken, she gets support from Daryl, and Rick gives in. He doesn't assert his will over the group, and his ego is not bruised. He may be reluctant, but he listens to this trusted, capable member of his team, his apocalypse family.

Treatment of Women

I'll beat you to death, Ed. I'll beat you to death.
–Shane to Ed Peletier, 103, "Tell It to the Frogs"

In our society, we are so inundated with images of violence against women, including the depravity of sex and violence mixed, that we barely acknowledge them anymore. From horror movies to *Criminal Minds* to *Law and Order: SVU* to the entire *CSI* franchise to images on the web, the media shows us women targeted because they are women.

It is a credit to the *TWD* writers and producers that when they have situations where violence against a woman is a possibility, they generally don't take us there. (At least not as of the end of Season 6, and I hope this will continue.) They don't wallow in the mire of this national pop-culture mud. Women are killed, sure. But only because they live in this high-mortality world; not because they are victimized as women.

In six seasons of a show about a violent, survival-oriented world, only twice have they shown a woman being hurt because she is a woman. The first time is in 103 when Ed hits his wife, Carol, and the other women in the camp. The second is when Maggie is accosted and threatened by the Governor in 307. In addition, anyone who has shown even an inclination to commit violence against women is dead now. Ed, Tony and Dave, the Governor, Pete, the Claimers—all dead.

It is Tony and Dave's attitude toward women that finalizes Rick's decision not to let them join the group. Dave is trying to convince Rick, Glenn, and Hershel to bring them back to the farm in 208, offering reminders that life on the road is fatal. Dave and Tony seem rough, but no more so than Daryl was in the beginning. Rick wants to say no, but he doesn't make it final until the following happens:

DAVE: *You got food, water?*
TONY: *You got any coos? Hadn't had a piece of ass in wee...*
DAVE: *Ah, listen, pardon my friend. City kids, they got no tact. No disrespect. So, listen, Glenn...*
RICK: *We've said enough.*

Dave knows very well that Tony's comment could be a deal breaker, and he is right. Rick hears it, turns his head ever so slightly toward Tony, and we know those two are never going to be on the farm. There is no way that the Rickites will allow anyone with that attitude to be in their company.

Even Deanna is not firm about caring for the women of Alexandria. She knows that Jessie is being hit by her husband, Pete, but she looks away because Pete is the town's only doctor. All she can manage when Rick brings it up is, "I hoped it'd get better." Really? That's it? For being a smart woman, she's not very smart. Rick thinks of a solution right away, which is to have Pete live in a separate house. When Deanna argues that Pete wouldn't put up with that, Rick says that if Pete doesn't comply, then they will kill him. A death sentence for wife abuse seems a bit much for our world, and this is a case where Morgan's cell could serve a purpose. But the point is that Rick is willing to do the right thing, show that abuse of women will not be tolerated, and trust that they will solve the problem of losing their doctor. (As it turns out, he is right because they have Denise.)

Even Shane, for all his problems, values the safety of women and defends them in 103. At the end of that episode, Ed comes down to the lakeside where Carol, Andrea, Amy and Jaqui are washing clothes. He lords it over the women, and when Andrea confronts him, he calls her an "uppity, smart-mouthed bitch." He orders Carol to leave with him, telling her, "You come on now, or you gonna regret it later?" The women tell her that she doesn't have to go and try to block Ed from reaching her, but he shoves them aside, hits Carol and starts to pull her away by the arm.

Shane sees this and strides over. He drags Ed away, throws him on the ground, kneels next to him and punches him repeatedly in the face, speaking fiercely:

> *You put your hands on your wife, your little girl, or anybody else in this camp one more time, I will not stop next time. Do you hear me? Do you hear me? I'll beat you to death, Ed. I'll beat you to death.*

It is one of the few times that we cheer for Shane. Not that wife abusers should be routinely beaten to a pulp, but how much would the rate of domestic violence drop if the good men in our world made it their business to not put up with it?

I think two things need to happen to significantly lower domestic violence rates. First, we need to raise our girls with such self-confidence (in who they are on the inside, not the outside) that men who are even controlling can't get a second date. And we need to raise our boys with such self-confidence (in who they are on the inside, not on the outside) that they don't feel such a need for control that they are willing to hit a woman in order to maintain it.

Second, we need good men to step up and voice their opposition when they know a woman is being abused. Men (speaking in generalities) tend to resist getting involved in each other's business. As Jim yells in 104 while criticizing Shane's punching of Ed, "That is their marriage, that is not his." But looking away when someone is being hurt allows the abuse to continue. It is a form of neutrality.

We need good men to come up with ways to express their disapproval of a man who is abusive. It could be simply verbal, with a group of the abuser's friends telling him they know what's going on and it's not okay. They could stop inviting him over to watch football, or to poker night or video game night or the golf foursome, or whatever else, and let him know exactly why. Those are just a couple of ideas.

It's risky—we never want to put a woman in more danger because her abusive partner learns that other people know. And an abused woman who isn't ready to change her situation may come to the defense of her own abuser, or like Carol, simply say that "it doesn't matter."

But even abandoning a "that's their business" attitude would open up pathways for solutions. And even having a good man be one of the people encouraging the abused woman to leave could help.

In the United States, abusers will be prosecuted if the wife brings charges, and we have shelters for women who are trying to get away from an abusive situation. But domestic violence is a silent crime that continues. We need to find more solutions, and good men are an integral part of that. We need you, guys. Please help us help our abused friends, sisters and daughters.

The predators in *TWD* abuse women. The Governor molests and threatens to rape Maggie, the Claimers attack any women they come across, and while we haven't seen it yet, I understand that Negan is no friend of women. For the Rickites, mistreatment of women is not acceptable in their group. What we are fighting for matters.

Freedom of Movement

He's one of mine; you have no claim on him.
—Dawn to Rick, 508, "Coda"

The boy wants to go home, so you have no claim on him.
—Rick to Dawn, 508, "Coda"

We saw how the predators in *TWD* don't let people leave. The opposite is true for the Rickites. The ability to come and go at will is a given for established members of Rick's group. Someone might be held for a temporary period if they are new to the group, such as when Michonne arrives. Rick tells her, "We can't let you go," but only to see if she is trustworthy.

Once that barrier is passed, going out alone might be ill-advised, but no one is stopped. Daryl often goes out looking for Sophia while they are at the farm. It is dangerous, but the others know that he is strong, and it is his decision. After the fall of Woodbury, Michonne goes out regularly to look for the Governor to make sure he is (un)dead, or to kill him if he isn't. When anybody sees her returning to the prison on her horse, they just ask how long she is staying this time.

And Carol decides to leave Alexandria permanently. She writes a note and leaves early in the morning before most people are awake, but not because she thinks she would be forcibly stopped. It is not an escape attempt—it is simply a decision to go on her own.

Freedom of movement is a basic right; otherwise people are prisoners in their own country. The Rickites (and the Hilltop, I am guessing) take freedom of movement as a given, and lead the way on this issue.

6

The Purpose-driven Apocalypse

A man who becomes conscious of the responsibility he bears toward a human being who affectionately waits for him, or to an unfinished work, will never be able to throw away his life. He knows the "why" for his existence, and will be able to bear almost any "how."
—Viktor E. Frankl, *Man's Search for Meaning*

Save the world for that little one. Save it for yourselves. Save it for the people out there who got nothin' left to do except survive.
—Abraham, 502, "Strangers"

The primary *TWD* purpose-driven character is, of course, Abraham. Ready to put a gun in his mouth after his wife and children are eaten by zombies, he is saved when he meets Eugene and takes on the mission of bringing this "scientist" to Washington to cure the apocalypse.

We all need a purpose, a reason for living. The good news is that we all have multiple purposes. They may be as a parent, a sibling, a child, or a friend. Our purpose may be contributing to a loved project, or sharing important messages with our community. The challenge in our world is when we think our purpose should be big and well-known. Abraham certainly does, and he has developed his own purpose hierarchy. When Glenn refuses to help them get to Washington until he finds Maggie, Abraham tells Tara in 411 that he admires Glenn's persistence, but "I don't know how else to say it. Saving the world is just, it's just more important."

Abraham goes through a very tough time when he finds out that Eugene isn't a scientist, and his big mission is based on a lie. But he comes out of it and finds other purposes in Alexandria. His big mission is replaced by missions to help his adopted community—building more walls, leading a construction crew, working with Sasha to lead walkers away from Alexandria. He also finds purpose in his love for Sasha, and in 616, he asks her about trying to have a baby. He tells Sasha, quoting her own line back to her, "Doing something as big as that— that's living." Starting a new life with her is his best new purpose.

Abraham finds new purpose in life because he routinely sets out to do things, to accomplish things. He volunteers for purpose. He doesn't shrink back, and he magnetizes purpose to himself. And he is flexible— ready to pitch in wherever he is needed. When we do this, there is always a mission in life, and life will always be meaningful.

Great Monologues

Michael Kudlitz does a wonderful job with Abraham's monologue at St. Sarah's church, trying to convince the Rickites to go to DC with him. He raises a toast to them for being survivors, then tells them it isn't enough.

Is that all you want to be? Wake up in the morning, fight the undead pricks, forage for food, go to sleep at night, two eyes open, rinse and repeat? You can do that. You got the strength, you got the skills. Thing is, for you people? For what you can do? Well that's just surrender.

It is one of the few times that Abraham abandons his profanity-laced, hysterically funny comments, and it is one of the moments where Michael shows to us another aspect of this wonderfully complex character—a damaged but sincere man beneath the raunchy remarks.

Furthermore, it could be that Abraham did have a big mission, but it wasn't what he thought. What if his big mission was to help Glenn find Maggie? What if little Maglee (the name fans have given to Glenn and Maggie's unborn baby) will grow up and cure the virus? Eugene, Abraham and Rosita were instrumental in bringing the Transitional World's First Couple back together, making it possible for Maglee to exist. If Maglee does become the One to Cure the Virus, then Abraham did save the world.

Abraham may not live to see Maglee's work, but Maggie (if she lives) may tell her child about this tall, strong, red-headed soldier who helped his father and mother find each other again.

Our purpose may be as part of a link in the chain, holding the chain of events together. Denise was killed, but not before she saved Carl's life. If Carl had died, Rick would probably have either lost any will to live or lost his integrity. Either he or his honor would have died. And if that happened to Rick, the Rickites might have fallen apart. Perhaps Negan or some other predator would win without Rick pulling everyone together. We will never know, but Denise was definitely an important link in the chain for Rick.

We may be serving an important purpose already, but not be aware of the value of our contributions. This is illustrated by Eugene, the cowardly lion of the Rickites, unaware of his own strength and courage. But Eugene had value all along. He knows how to filter creek water for drinking, he knows how to pick locks—very valuable in a world of scavenging for food and medicine. He knows how to keep the solar panels going in Alexandria. Eugene always had those skills, but he didn't have the self-worth to say, "Hey, I know how to get into locked houses and provide safe drinking water." He felt he had to lie about who he was in order to get the group to protect him, but that was never true.

Eugene finally does come around to believing in himself; he creates the recipe for making bullets with full knowledge of how valuable this is. The lesson here is that we all have gifts to offer, and people will care for us even if we aren't the biggest, the strongest, or shoot the straightest. Every community needs a wide variety of talents.

It is fine if we don't have a big purpose, if we don't see big results, if our purpose is different than what we think it is, or if we are just a link in the chain. Because being a link, holding tight to each other, helping forge the bonds with each other, that's pretty damn cool. It's a pretty good takeaway for a little road trip called life.

6

The Apocalypse is Happening to Everyone: In Honor of Erin

Take what you need and God Bless.
—Sign in pharmacy window, 204, "Cherokee Rose"

In literature, film, and television, the story is sometimes told so that we have sympathy for the main characters and forget about everyone else. We definitely root for the main characters in *TWD*, but the creators never let us forget that the apocalypse is also happening to people we will never meet. We see this in the messages that humans leave behind for each other.

In 204, when Maggie and Glenn go to the abandoned pharmacy, there is a sign in the window: "Take what you need and God Bless." Whoever left it didn't have to do that; people would have seen the abandoned pharmacy and taken items anyway. But this good person wanted to communicate with anyone who came to the pharmacy. Leaving the sign was a gift—a great act of kindness reminding people that humanity and goodwill still exist. These types of messages are a lifeline for the *TWD* inhabitants, and for us.

In 312, Rick, Michonne, and Carl pass a sign that says, "Erin, we tried for Stone Mountain. J." Is this a family that got separated? A best friend? A neighbor or coworker who the writers of the sign were trying to save? In any case, it is a mark of humanity and caring, still alive and well. Sadly, later in the episode, when Rick's car is stopped and surrounded by walkers, one walker banging on the window has a bracelet with the letters E-R-I-N. We never see Erin in human form, but we know somebody cared for her.

On the road after Woodbury, the Governor sees a barn with writing all over the side. There are messages to Brian Heriot, telling him the writers love him and where to meet them; there are messages saying that Chad Krear died, that Negan Cook died, that someone found Ken Jones, letting Casey Brewer know where to meet his friends or family, and telling Mollica it is not safe to come home. We never know any of these people, but we know the people writing these words were desperately trying to communicate with the people they loved. The apocalypse is happening to everyone.

Other tributes to humanity are made by the former human that Abraham and Sasha find when they take shelter in an insurance office. The insurance company owner was bitten, locked himself in a room with a glass wall and wrote a message on a whiteboard before he died.

Proud to have provided value
I pray for the world
Keep going
Stay cheerful
The bite kill

We know this man is ex-military, because Abraham finds a jacket with multiple medals on it in a closet. The man knew what would happen after he died, but not that a shot in the head would prevent the turn. So he locked himself in the room to stop himself from hurting anyone. He died as he lived—protecting people.

Abraham retrieves the jacket and puts it on; but before he does, he removes the medals. He shows his basic honesty by not acquiring medals that he didn't earn (unlike the Governor, who acquired Brian Heriot's identity). Abraham won't steal another man's accomplishments. He honors the man's humanity, even though the man is a walker now.

The Rickites put out their own messages, such as "Glenn, go to Terminus. Maggie, Sasha, Bob." Anyone else coming across this wouldn't know any of these people, but they would be reminded that there are people still out there, still trying to help each other. The most poignant, of course, is "Sophia, stay here. We will come every day." As with Erin, the effort doesn't work. But it reminds any passersby that people are still being people. And the *TWD* writers remind us of the same thing.

The apocalypse is happening to everyone on *TWD*. In our world, challenges are happening to everyone. We have both global and personal apocalypses. Whether we leave messages on physical walls or write electronic messages viewed in little boxes, they still mean the same thing. I am here. I want to reach you. Let's find a way to connect, please.

If *The Walking Dead* tells us anything, it is that we need each other. That's easy to forget in our world, where we can survive in solitude. But even though we may survive on our own, we will never thrive. We need each other to get through the rough times and to celebrate the good times. People are here to help us grow; sometimes through encouragement and sometimes through challenge. Everyone in our life serves a purpose, and our strongest growth comes when we work on being the best person we can be in our relationships. While time alone is important and can be rejuvenating and healing, trying to make it alone or avoiding personal contact with other people won't fill or open anyone's heart.

In addition, it is good to have people in our lives who think the way we do, as well as people who don't think like we do. Society needs people of all skills, personalities and talents. We need people who are strong and willing to fight when necessary, people who are intellectual, and people who are gentle. We need people who know who they are, and sometimes people who don't know who they are, to show us every stage along the path. We need people who are opinionated and people who just don't want to get involved. Every person is a teacher, and sometimes the people who annoy us the most are the best teachers of all, because they show us where we need to smooth out our own rough spots. We are here to grow, to empathize, and to let go of negative emotions. Every step we take along this path will help us to be closer with others and to find our own best self. Or, as Glenn puts it, "We can make it together, but we can *only* make it together."

TWD shines a light on these lessons, and for that, we can be grateful. So be well, my fellow fans. Live, grow, laugh, and sit down by a tree to have a good cry every now and then. Find your fellow travelers on the journey. Find the people with whom you want to talk about your day and share mints in the evening, confide in when you're feeling scared, eat chocolate pudding, plan future adventures, fight for positive principles, pray, and celebrate small, daily victories. No matter how bad the world looks, I still believe there's a purpose; I still believe there's a reason. Even a messed-up world will eventually get better.

About the Author

Susan Lehman is a huge fan of *The Walking Dead*. In her life outside of *TWD*, Susan has worked in politics, higher education, on film crews and in real estate. She also acted and directed in theatre for fifteen years, and her personal interests include gardening and learning about religion and history. Politically, she is a registered Independent who leans libertarian, and spiritually she is non-denominational, but has a strong belief in God. Susan lives in a small town in Pennsylvania.

Printed in Great Britain
by Amazon